IRREPLACEABLE

IRREPLACEABLE

A Father's Guide
to Raising
World Changers

ALLEN HICKMAN

Irreplaceable: A Father's Guide to Raising World Changers
Copyright © 2019 Allen Hickman

Published by: Inprov Ltd., Southlake, TX
2150 E. Continental Blvd.
Southlake, TX 76092

All rights reserved under International Copyright Law. Contents and/or cover may not be reproduced in whole or in part in any form without the express written consent of the Publisher.

Unless otherwise noted, all scripture quotations are taken from the Holy Bible, New International Version®, NIV®. Copyright © 1973, 1978, 1984, 2011 by Biblica, Inc.™ Used by permission of Zondervan. All rights reserved worldwide. www.zondervan.com The "NIV" and "New International Version" are trademarks registered in the United States Patent and Trademark Office by Biblica, Inc.™

Scripture quotations marked (AMP) are taken from the Amplified® Bible, Copyright © 2015 by The Lockman Foundation. Used by permission. www.Lockman.org

Scripture quotations marked (AMPC) are taken from the Amplified Bible, Copyright © 1954, 1958, 1962, 1964, 1965, 1987 by The Lockman Foundation. Used by permission.

Scriptures quotations marked (ESV) are taken from the English Standard Version® (ESV®). Copyright © 2001 by Crossway, a publishing ministry of Good News Publishers. All rights reserved.

Scripture quotations marked (NKJV) are taken from the New King James Version®. Copyright © 1982 by Thomas Nelson. Used by permission. All rights reserved.

Scripture quotations marked (NLT) are taken from the Holy Bible, New Living Translation, Copyright © 1996, 2004, 2015 by Tyndale House Foundation. Used by permission of Tyndale House Publishers, Inc., Carol Stream, Illinois 60188. All rights reserved.

ISBN: 978-1-7327904-9-0
Printed in the USA.

This book is dedicated to:

My wonderful wife, Amy.
You are truly the love of my life and the most godly person I have ever met.

My wonderful boys, you have made my life so much better.

To Uncle Bill—thanks for the push!

Praise for *Irreplaceable*

Irreplaceable: this is how my friend Allen Hickman describes a godly father. A father of 11 boys, Allen gives practical examples and biblical advice to help dads launch their children successfully and fulfill God's kingdom purpose. He notes, "Our country has lost its sense of character because fathers aren't around anymore to give it to their children and model it in front of them, but I believe we can change that. I believe you can change that." Like Allen, I believe we can change that, too. If fathers would apply the wisdom Allen shares in these pages, it would undoubtedly change the direction of families and churches everywhere.

JAMES ROBISON – Founder and President,
LIFE Outreach International, Fort Worth, Texas

Before reading a book, you want to know how credible the author writing it is. This is especially true if the book is on parenting. There are so many opinions out there on how to raise children. I am sure that we as parents didn't get it all right either. That is why I was so excited to hear that Allen Hickman had decided to write a book on being a father. Not only is Allen the father of 11 boys…he is a dad! There's a huge difference between the two. As a dad, mentor, coach, and godly example to his boys, Allen has something to say to all of us. His sons are a testimony of the fact that relational parenting really works. I highly recommend *Irreplaceable* to parents and grandparents alike. The truths and heartwarming stories will challenge you to take your parenting—discipleship in the home—to a new level!

> **MARK JOBE** – Campus Pastor, Gateway Church, Southlake, Texas

Raising children could be the most important yet most difficult job on the planet. Many books are published each year on parenting, written by 'experts' who can't seem to agree with other 'experts' on the best way to parent children. *Irreplaceable* by Allen Hickman could be the book parents have been looking for. It is a biblically-based book that is refreshing in its honesty and vulnerability, with stories that are down-to-earth and inspiring. I've known the Hickmans for a long time and have observed that they walk their talk. Allen and his wife, Amy, have parented 11 sons in a way that has inspired all of them to respect, honor, and deeply love their parents. That's probably the best endorsement a book on raising children could ever get. I highly recommend this book.

> **E. WAYNE DRAIN** – Author, Pastor, Songwriter, and Founder of Wayne Drain Ministries

Fatherhood is one of the most important roles anyone on earth can play. I mean, why else would God himself relate to us in this way?

Unfortunately, because of the importance of fathers, we have watched the enemy attack them incessantly, threatening the future of families, communities, and ultimately, our nation. The problem is, many of us have never been shown how to approach fatherhood from a biblical perspective—in a way that works!

There's no better man to guide us in this area than Pastor Allen Hickman. As a father of 11 God-loving sons, he has led each of them in a way that all men can learn from. As his friend, I have watched him parent "with a vision," teaching his children important lessons such as: security, identity, integrity, and love. He's also one of the best coaches on the dreaded "d" word—*discipline*!

With the lessons taught in this book, I am confident that each of us can become more godly and confident fathers and leaders in our home. We can live in such a way that our kids, like Allen's, will become "arrows in the hands of a warrior!"

>**PASTOR JIM GRAFF** – Pastor of Faith Family Church in Victoria, Virginia and President of Significant Church Network

Having known my friend Allen Hickman for so many years now, I loved reading this book! I have laughed out loud with this great family many times! Picture this: Allen up on a dresser hiding from his boys! Then, after laughing one minute, I have been struck by the sheer grace it would take to raise 11 boys. Every once in a while, there's a book that comes at the right time for the church and for a culture that's come untied from its moorings.

Living in an inner-city culture for the past thirty-five years, I've had plenty of opportunity to see the ugly effects of a fatherless generation. The media would have you believe that it's guns or trash in the streets, or even drugs, that are the cause of these families collapsing.

As Allen has said so well and demonstrated by being the great father he is to these boys becoming men—fathers are *irreplaceable*! Do yourself or your church a favor and order a book for each father in your life. This is a Malachi 4:6 promise.

BART PIERCE – Senior Pastor of Rock City Church, Baltimore, Maryland

TABLE OF CONTENTS

Introduction

Chapter 1:	Why Vision Is so Important	6
Chapter 2:	Develop a Vision for Your Family	20

Section 1 – Who Are You?

Chapter 3:	Assess Your Children's Value	32
Chapter 4:	Understand Your Children's Destiny	44
Chapter 5:	Build a Secure Foundation	56

Section 2 – Let's Talk About Love

Chapter 6:	Let Them Know They're Special	72
Chapter 7:	Love Is Spelled T-I-M-E	80
Chapter 8:	Create Life Through Your Words	90
Chapter 9:	The What and Why of Discipline	98
Chapter 10:	How to Discipline	112
Chapter 11:	Destructive Worldviews in Discipline	126

Section 3 – Developing Real Character

Chapter 12:	Take Responsibility	140
Chapter 13:	Never Quit. Persevere	150
Chapter 14:	Integrity Starts Young	156
Chapter 15:	Deal with Failure	166

Section 4 – Built for Purpose

Chapter 16:	Help Them Launch	178
Chapter 17:	Your Children Are World Changers	190
Chapter 18:	Create a Rite of Passage	200

Conclusion: Final Thoughts

INTRODUCTION

As a father, you are irreplaceable. That may sound strange to you, especially since fatherhood is something that many guys feel happens "to" them. One day they're romancing their wife, then nine months later, they suddenly have a lifetime of responsibility laying on their shoulders.

On top of that, this world seems to constantly play down—or completely dismiss—the role of "Dad" in our society. Culture tells us that a family can look like just about anything you can imagine and that a father is expendable.

I'm here to tell you, that couldn't be further from the truth.

Your family needs you to step up and be the man God has called you to be. I'm sure that even as you read that last sentence, something inside you is shouting, "Yes!" But it can be terrifying to stand up and take that responsibility.

When, on June 12, 1988, I became a first-time father, I had no idea that this journey of fatherhood would take me to depths that I didn't know existed and heights I could only dream about. You probably feel the same way.

If you're like me, you may have felt ill-prepared for the job. Statistically, you probably still do. Let me tell you, having more children doesn't make it any easier. After our second son was born, the Lord spoke to us and told us we would have "a lot of children." My wife and I thought "a lot" would be *maybe* four. Neither of us imagined we would have *eleven* sons. Yes, you read that right…Eleven! Obviously our definition of "a lot" was different than God's!

We also didn't expect that at one point we'd have seven boys under 10 years old. If you think you're in a predicament, just take a moment to let *that* sink in!

Through it all, one truth became clear to me: anybody can make a baby, but it takes someone special to be a *dad*… and I wanted to be a good one. Because you've picked up this book, I'm betting you do, too.

As a pastor, I have seen the devastation that people walk through daily because they didn't have a father, or because they had a hurtful, abusive father, or because they had a father who simply didn't care. I've seen the struggles they've gone through firsthand, and how our heavenly Father wanted to help them.

Because of that, when I became a father, I started praying daily, asking God to show me how to be a good father. I asked Him what I could do to give my boys everything they needed to be great men. I asked Him to show me how to live a life that inspires them to never settle for less. I asked Him to show me what to say, or do, that would challenge them to be men who would change the world.

Through these pages run the lessons that I have learned from God and from my boys. As you read, I hope you hear the heart of a man who desperately loves his children and realizes that the world is fighting for their souls.

If we want our children to become men and women of purpose, we have to learn to fight and rally against everything the world throws at them. It's a battle we can't afford to lose, and we need the Lord to win it.

Together, we're going to see just how important a dad's role is in this day and age, and why you can't simply "phone it in" or only be the guy who delivers the family a paycheck. More than anything, you'll see that your children *need* you to be an active part of their lives. Every day.

Your role as father isn't something you've fallen into by accident. It's a calling; it's not an option. Your children need you.

You, Dad, are *Irreplaceable!*

1

Why Vision Is so Important

*Like arrows in the hands of a warrior
are children born in one's youth.
Blessed is the man whose quiver is full of them...*
(Psalm 127:4-5)

When my boys were young, I wanted to teach them a sport we could enjoy together for years to come—something we could still do once getting tackled and running bases at full speed were no longer fun. With that vision before me, I started teaching them golf.

It wasn't long before I realized I had nine boys but only six sets of golf clubs. Even my lefty had to play as a righty. One day, as I sat in my quiet time, I got angry about the situation. "God, You gave me these nine kids and said You would help take care of them. How in the world am I going to support them through college if I can't even afford enough golf clubs for all of them?!"

I slammed my Bible shut and walked out of my quiet time.

It may surprise you to find out I talk to God like that, but I figure if it's in my heart, He already knows. I might as well be honest about it.

Later that day, I was playing golf with four of my boys when a man walked out to the fifteenth hole. He said, "You don't know me, but this morning for some reason you came to my mind. I make golf clubs. Does one of your children need golf clubs?"

"Yes, he does," I said. Clearly, God had spoken to this man at the same time I was yelling at Him about not providing.

"I have a left-handed set ready to go," he said. "Is one of your kids left-handed?"

I said, "Yes, sir, he is."

He told me to come by when we finished playing.

Later, as we headed out of the club, the golf course manager, who was cleaning out a shed, flagged us down.

"Hey, Brother Allen! Come over here for a minute! We were cleaning out some old lockers this morning and found two sets of children's golf clubs. We were talking about who to give them to and you immediately came to my mind. Would you like to have them?"

Shocked, I said. "Yes, I'd love to have them."

I collected all the clubs and picked up my other children. We returned to the club to hit golf balls together with our new clubs. As I watched all my boys practicing their swings, I cried for yelling at God about not providing only hours earlier. I swear I heard Him laughing. It was as if He was saying, "Allen, I got this."

I learned a valuable lesson that day: *God doesn't provide for wondering: He provides for vision.* That provision—that miracle—didn't happen by accident. It happened because I had a vision, one God helped me develop for my family: to find a sport we could play together for years to come. It was a simple vision, but God provided for it—because He always provides for the vision, no matter how small it may seem to be at the time.

Soon He helped me develop an even wider vision for our family—and in doing so has made such a life-changing difference for us that I want every dad to understand the power behind having a vision for his family.

Why am I speaking specifically to dads? Because I believe dads are the originators of vision for their family. Don't get me wrong, moms are important. They help support and implement the vision, but dads are responsible for developing and initiating it.

That's why, Dad, it's time to step up.

What is Vision?

Vision isn't like making a New Year's resolution. It's not simply hoping you can meet a goal or change a habit.

Vision is about setting specific direction for your family.

It's about prayerfully identifying what you want your life, each of your children's lives, and your family as a whole to be.

Of course, you don't need to know every detail about what the future holds, but you do need to know where your family is headed.

The verse at the top of this chapter, Psalm 127:4, says, "Like arrows in the hands of a warrior are children..." What a profound statement about children and parenting: *children are arrows.* Our job is to aim them in the direction of their destinies and then let them go as they spring toward it.

> Raising a family without vision
> is like shooting an arrow without aiming.

Notice I said you must "aim" them. If you fail to aim an arrow, there's almost no chance it will hit the target, no matter how hard you pull the string. Raising a family without vision is like shooting an arrow without aiming.

No matter how much you want them to succeed, a lack of direction in their lives will undoubtedly hinder their journeys. You need a target for your family and your kids. You need a vision.

Even nature gives us a lesson in vision. Each year, salmon swim upstream. They don't know what rocks or hills they'll encounter, but they know, without a doubt, the direction they're going; and they don't stop until they get there. They don't swim upstream for exercise. It's their vision of being able to reproduce in calm waters that causes them to push through. If they were to accept the current of life that was coming against them, they would never make it to a more desired destination.

The same is true for us. We all want good things in life—a good marriage, thriving children, a family that loves each other and gets along—but those things don't happen by accident. They all require vision to be able to see the destination upstream and a willingness to fight to get there.

We live in a go-with-the-flow society. The path of least resistance is often the most attractive. You'll never put in the work to swim upstream unless you see the destination clearly for both you and your family. That's the reward of having a vision.

Vision Gives Direction

Over the years, I've discovered the importance of vision. It makes life—and parenting—easier, more fruitful, and more enjoyable. It helps you stay focused because you have an end goal. When opportunities arise or decisions need to be made with regard to your children or your family, vision helps simplify the decision-making process. You don't have strain or stress. You don't have to worry about what to do.

Sometimes you don't even have to talk about it. Vision makes all the decisions for you.

Let me give you an illustration. If I want to visit New Orleans, which is due south on I-59 from our home in Picayune, Mississippi, I can drive from wherever I am in the city and get to the interstate without even thinking about it. I don't have to fight any considerations about going north, and I never worry about which way to turn when I arrive at an intersection. Why?

Because I know where I'm going. I have a vision.

If I hop in my car and start driving without a vision, every intersection becomes a major decision, every crossroad becomes a debate.

The same is true in parenting. As a dad, you must have a clear vision for your family, so you always know exactly where you're headed and how to handle the twists and turns of parenthood.

Sadly, many fathers set the bar far too low...or they don't set a bar at all. I have heard parents say, "Well, my kids didn't get pregnant or do drugs, so I guess I did something right." What a pathetic vision! In fact, that's not really vision at all, is it? That's simply a breath of relief that they didn't mess them up that badly! But you don't have to live like that, hoping that everything turns out all right in the end. You can help set their course.

Just to be clear, I'm not suggesting it's a parent's job to determine their child's purpose or what job they'll have when they grow up. I am talking about training them to be the kind of men and women you want them to be, to help mold them into what they'll look like in this society. When you do that, things like finding an occupation will take care of itself.

You can raise children who love the Lord, impact the world for His glory, and are a blessing to you and your spouse. Our verse refers to children as "arrows in the hands of a warrior." They *are* arrows, and you—their father—are the warrior. You are to release your children toward their destiny, and it starts when they're young.

Vision is Practical

You'll never hear me say my children are perfect. You'll also never hear me say what I'm suggesting is easy. Far from it. Believe me, I've had to go to my fair share of parent-teacher conferences. Time and again, my children have pushed me and my wife to our limits. But every time that happened, we stayed faithful to the vision that had already been set in motion. Step by step, we kept pressing toward that vision, doing what we knew we had to do. That's real life!

Having 11 boys close together presented a myriad of parenting challenges. One of those challenges was going out to eat. Before I was married, I had been in restaurants where kids were out of control, running around, and making the staff and other guests angry. When I started having more and more kids, I knew my crew would be at risk of doing the same thing if I didn't take action. So, I stated a vision: I wanted to be able to take our kids anywhere without it turning into chaos. To accomplish that, Amy and I had to do a few things. For starters, we made sure that when we were at home, we sat down together for family meals. That provided an atmosphere where we could train them on how to act, and correct behaviors that we knew wouldn't be acceptable in a public setting.

Was it fun going through that training process with 11 children? No! Would it have been easier to throw our hands up and let them do whatever they wanted? Absolutely! But our vision wouldn't allow it. It dictated which actions we needed to take. Because we wanted to arrive at our goal, we took the necessary steps to get there. The vision made decisions for us.

My wife and I also had a vision that our children would make their world a better place—no matter where they found themselves in the future. Quite often I would take my boys to help people move, deliver groceries to the hungry, go on mission trips, or other character-building activities. After all, to make a difference, one has to be a servant. The vision I had for my boys to improve the world around them required that I teach them how to serve.

WHY VISION IS SO IMPORTANT

Another of our stated visions for my boys is that they would love and cherish the Word of God. To press toward that vision, three to five times a week I gathered all the boys in the living room for Family Time. We'd sit down and I'd have each one list something they were thankful for. Then I would read the Bible to them before they went to bed. I made the Word of God a part of our life because that was part of our vision. These weren't activities we were necessarily doing before we had a vision...but once we did, the vision made the decisions about what to do for us.

From Jacob, my third oldest son:

> *Even as a married man, I still remember gathering four or five nights a week in my parents' living room at the end of the day, right before bedtime. Dad would call, "Boys, y'all come in here."*
>
> *All my brothers and I would come out from whatever room we were in at the time to sit in a circle on the ground, on couches, and on laps for "Family Time." My dad would always start by reading a short passage of Scripture. Being a preacher, he showed great restraint by rarely taking much time to explain everything about the scripture or what it meant, even though he knew all that. He just read it to us and offered a sentence or two afterward such as, "This is who we are as Hickmans," and "Always fight to live like that." Then dad would go*

around the whole room and one by one he would ask us what we were thankful for.

Thinking about it now, with an audience of 8–12 people, that was our first exposure to public speaking. It's where we became comfortable speaking in front of others. We all have many fond memories from Family Time over the years, from funny stories about things that happened that day to laughing at the three-year-old who's thankful for Cheetos.

Family Time was an integral part of my life growing up. I can't wait to have my own Family Time when my wife and I have kids of our own.

Vision Brings Restraint

The Bible says, "Where there is no vision, the people perish" (Proverbs 29:18). The word *perish* in that verse could also be translated as *unrestrained*. In other words, where there is no vision, people are unrestrained. People *need* restraint. I'm not talking about the kind of restraint that chains provide. I'm talking about the kind of restraint that traffic lanes provide. Traffic lanes are a form of restraint, but they keep you on the road so you can get to your destination. Being unrestrained draws a picture of going here and there, or whichever way feels right at the moment, never getting anywhere.

The Lord taught me about this using a map in the back

WHY VISION IS SO IMPORTANT

of the Bible that showed the wanderings of Israel. The book of Exodus tells the account of when God used Moses to set His people free from slavery to Egypt. With mighty miracles, He led them out of captivity with the promise of bringing them into a land of their very own. However, when Israel finally arrived at the Promised Land, they were so afraid of its inhabitants that they refused to enter it. Because they didn't trust God, they walked away from their planned destination and began living without a destination at all. For the next 40 years they wandered...and that's a perfect representation of what it's like to live a life without vision (see the arrows below). There's a lot of movement without heading toward a destination!

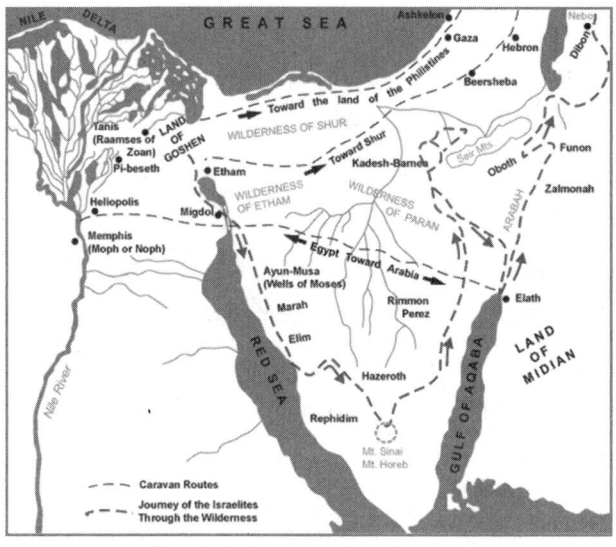

Source: https://www.bible-history.com/maps/route_exodus.html

The same can happen with our children if we raise them without a vision. They can grow up wandering, without really getting to where we would have liked for them to go. Without vision, they're destined to repeat mistakes from the past and get nowhere at all.

Vision Brings Blessing

For many fathers, examining their marriage, family, and how they're raising their kids is like finding themselves lost in a dark hole. It doesn't have to be like that. I want you to know that with a vision, you can lead yourself, your family, and future generations out of that hole. You can take you and your family from wherever you are to wherever God's called you to be.

Family is supposed to be a blessing. God was the One who created family. No matter where you are from or what you have been through, you can develop a concrete vision and put your family on a fulfilling new path.

My hope is that your vision will be the first step to helping your children fulfill the purpose and destiny God has for each of them. Remember, you are the warrior; they are the arrows. It's time to shoot them toward their destiny—a process that begins with vision. Let's get started.

Key Points

1. Vision is essential. If you don't know where you're going, then every crossroad becomes a major decision.
2. Your vision for your children will dictate how you parent.
3. Developing a vision for your family will result in an easier, more fruitful, and more enjoyable life. It's the difference between letting life happen to you and you proactively advancing through it.
4. The Bible refers to children as "arrows in the hands of a warrior." Parents are called to "aim" them toward their target (their destiny).

Discussion Questions

1. What's your definition of vision?
2. Why is vision important, even for families?
3. What vision do you currently have for your family?
4. What vision do you currently have for your children?

Take Action

Grab a piece of paper and take a few moments to write down the types of things you'd like to see in a vision for your family. How do you want your children to act? What kind of atmosphere do you want in your house? What character attributes are most important for your children to have by the time they leave your house? What other thoughts come to mind?

2

Develop a Vision for Your Family

The LORD had said to Abram, "Go from your country, your people and your father's household to the land I will show you. I will make you into a great nation, and I will bless you; I will make your name great, and you will be a blessing. I will bless those who bless you, and whoever curses you I will curse; and all peoples on earth will be blessed through you."
(Genesis 12:1-3)

Many parents allow the vision for their families to be dictated to them by the world. Unfortunately, the world has no shortage of bad advice. Television doctors and talking heads love to tell us how to spend time with our children, how we should and shouldn't discipline, how to raise our kids, how to feed our children, how to play with our children, and more.

The problem with this advice is that it's only worth what you pay for it. It's so-called "wisdom" that changes like the wind. The advice spouted as rock solid 20 years ago isn't the same advice proclaimed today. While many experts have the best of intentions, they are not the creators of vision—God is. And when it comes to your family, He is the authority you want to listen to.

Step 1: Go to the Creator

If you're ready to create a vision for your family, the first—and most important—step is to go to the Creator. In Genesis 12, God told Abram to leave his homeland. God promised that if Abram would do that, He'd take him somewhere good and bless the whole world through him. That's not a vision Abram could've come up with on his own. Abram had to get his vision from the God who created him. The same is true for you. If you'll follow the Lord, He'll give you a vision—for yourself, for your family, and for your children—that's bigger and better than you could ever imagine on your own.

Sometimes people believe that if they start following God and seeking His vision, He will make them do something they'll hate. Nothing could be further from the truth! God has put specific talents and personality traits within you; and if you'll let Him, He'll use them in amazing ways.

God will provide a vision for your family and your children if you're willing to hear it.

This is step one: *begin praying.* Seek the Lord and ask Him to help you develop a vision. When I felt the Lord leading me to set a vision, I got away and sought the Lord for my family.

DEVELOP A VISION FOR YOUR FAMILY

I prayed that the Lord would help our family to be a sweet aroma to His nose, a joy to His eyes, and bring glory to His name in all things. It didn't take long before the words started coming to me. The Lord was faithful to help me develop a vision for my family that has guided our daily lives. And what He did for my family, He'll do for yours, too.

It's important to note here that when you're asking God for a vision, you've got to be confident that He'll speak to you. The Bible promises that "My sheep hear my voice" (John 10:27). He will speak to you, but it most likely won't be in an audible voice. God frequently speaks to me through His Word and my thoughts as I'm going through life. If you'll pay attention, I promise God will take every opportunity to speak to you, too. As a lover of movies, God has spoken to me countless times through lines that I hear on screen. He uses them to immediately impress something on my heart. The key to remember is that God's given you the responsibility of raising your children. And if He's given you the responsibility, He will certainly tell you what you need to know to do it well.

Step 2: Trust What the Lord Has Already Said

God has already given us insight into who He is, what He wants for His people, and what He expects from us. We only need to read and study His Word to learn what He's already said.

For example, Genesis 2:24 says, "That is why a man leaves his father and mother and is united to his wife, and they become one flesh." That tells me that my wife and I are one. We don't need to live at odds with one another.

Proverbs 18:22 says, "*Whoso* findeth a wife findeth a *good thing*, and obtaineth favour of the LORD" (KJV, emphasis mine). Therefore, I know God doesn't want me looking around for a replacement wife or complaining about the one He's given me. I need to come alongside the Word of God and recognize that on January 3, 1987, I found "a good thing."

You may be thinking, *Allen, the Word of God may say I have a good thing, but this marriage isn't good. In fact, it's far from good!* If that's the case, then you have yet another reason to create a vision that can dictate your decisions, actions, and attitudes. Walk toward the vision with everything you have and ask God to show you how to make your marriage the best it can be.

Sure, challenges will come; but with a vision, you and your family won't stay in that quagmire. Instead, you'll keep going after the end goal. You'll keep believing and saying that you and your family are going somewhere because that's what families with vision do.

Step 3: Look Forward

The third step in developing a vision is to look forward. You'll never find a vision in your rearview mirror. You need to start fresh. That means you might need to forgive those who have hurt or disappointed you. You may need to let go of past mistakes—yours and others. If you want a vision for the future, you can't keep looking back at the past. The past is over. Let it die. Forgive and move on.

The same goes for your children. Don't let their past mistakes cause you to undercut your vision for them or classify them as "bad." If you identify one as "the bad child", I promise you that he'll live up to that. Look forward to a better future for each of your children, one that focuses on pulling out the good that's in each one rather than calling out the bad.

Step 4: Walk in What You Know

In Genesis 12, when God called Abram out of his homeland, Abram didn't know where he was going. All he knew to do was to start. That's all you can do, too. Start where you are and finish each step. You may want Him to show you the whole picture, but guess what? He doesn't do that! He shows you one step at a time. Once you finish that first step, He'll show you the next, and then the next.

As I've said—and I'll say again—my children aren't perfect. Yours may be, but mine didn't come ready-made like that. However, by developing a vision, I have shot each of my "arrows" in the direction the Lord gave to me, and it's made a world of difference.

Put the steps I've shared here into practice and allow the Lord to help you develop a detailed vision for your family. Go to the Creator. Trust in what He has already said. Look forward. And walk in what you know, one step at a time. As you do, let this be the beginning of a new season—a new life—for your family. Let it be one where you are aiming your children toward their future!

Key Points

1. God, not man, is the creator of vision. Go to Him for your vision.
2. The Word of God provides insight into who God is and what He wants for you. Study His Word to know what He says about you, your family, your children, and how He wants you to live your life.
3. Forgiveness and letting go of the past are essential steps for moving forward in your vision.
4. God doesn't reveal every step of your vision at the start. It comes one step at a time. As each step is completed, He reveals the next.

Discussion Questions

1. What has the Lord revealed to you through His Word about your vision?
2. What things, situations, or people in your past do you need to forgive or let go of?
3. What vision has the Lord revealed to you so far?
4. What is your first step in bringing that vision to pass?

Take Action

Take out the sheet of paper you wrote on after reading the first chapter and prayerfully look at what you wrote down. Ask the Lord what needs to stay, what needs to go, and what needs to be added. Then set an appointment for yourself to get away for a few hours (at least) where you can be alone and develop a vision for your family. There's no formula here, no right or wrong way to do it. What's important is that it includes the outcomes you want to see most for your family and your children. Your vision should detail what kind of people you want your children to become and what overall values and activities your family is going to embrace to make sure those arrows straighten up and fly right.

SECTION 1
WHO ARE YOU?

In this fatherless world, many people are searching for something...anything. They don't know who they are, what they're supposed to be, how they are supposed to act, or what is expected of them. In that environment, people are relegated to living by their feelings, going along with what feels right at the moment. What a disaster! God never intended men and women to live so aimlessly.

He wants you to know who you are and where you come from. He wants you to feel the power of a destiny and know what is expected of that destiny. He wants you to walk with a sense of purpose and confidence, and be secure enough to take chances in life because you know who you are.

Part of the reason we're seeing this aimlessness in our society is because we as men and fathers have neglected one of our fundamental roles. In fact, it was our *first* role. The first job God gave man is missed by most people who read the Bible. Genesis 2:19 states, "God brought every animal to Adam to see what he would call them. And whatever Adam called each living creature, that was its name."

From the beginning God anointed man to give animals their identity. As fathers, we still have that anointing on us. We have the ability to show and convince our children who they are. Let's not squander this responsibility. It's one of the most important roles we have, and it affects them every single day for the rest of their lives.

3

Assess Your Children's Value

I praise you because I am fearfully and wonderfully made;
your works are wonderful, I know that full well.
(Psalm 139:14)

Early one morning, my wife called me in a panic. While wandering around our yard, my four-year-old son had found a machete stuck in the ground. It had been left there by one of his older brothers. You can imagine what happened next. I could follow his path all around the yard. He hacked down bushes and took chunks out of poles and trees. Finally, he made it to our water well. A hard rain had uncovered the main water line coming into the house, leaving a four-foot section exposed. It was the perfect target.

He came running into the house a few minutes later. "Mommy, come look what I made for you!" he cheered.

He ran back out of the house and stood in front of the fountain of water spraying 20 feet into the air. The sun was high, and the light filtered through it to create a rainbow. It was quite a sight. He held his hands up high and said, "I made you a fountain!"

Our little boy—in complete innocence and total joy—thought he'd made something beautiful; but in the process, he had cut off life-giving water to the house. He celebrated something we didn't need, clueless about what was really important. He simply hadn't yet learned the proper value of things.

Children need to be taught, shown, and convinced of what is valuable and what is not. They come into this world confused and unaware of what is truly important. We have a fatherless generation racing around spending all their time, money, and efforts on what is not valuable and giving little time to what is truly priceless.

....

> Let them [your children] know that God was there at their conception, putting good things inside their DNA and forming them into original works of art. Then show them where He states in His Word that not only was He there at their beginning but also that He has good thoughts and plans for their future.

....

Have you ever paid way too much for something and then realized its real value? You know that sinking feeling you get when you finally realize its true worth? I see that a lot in older people. They say things like, "If I had it to do over again," or, "I wish I could go back..."

Often, their words are an admission that they have spent their lives focused on things that they now realize aren't valuable. Unfortunately, it's impossible to go back in life, so we need to get our values right the first time. When your children are able to properly assess true value—of themselves, of their destiny, and of the world around them—their lives will be so much better, and their decisions will be so much easier to make.

Understanding Their Own Value

The first value your children need to learn is the value of their own lives. I always tell my children, "You are a one-of-a-kind masterpiece." That's a statement I encourage you to repeat over and over again to your children, too.

The Word of God declares this truth in Psalm 139. Let them know that God was there at their conception, putting good things inside their DNA and forming them into original works of art. Then show them where He states in His Word that not only was He there at their beginning, but also that He has good thoughts and plans for their future. Even science proclaims this with the uniqueness of fingerprints and DNA.

Tell each of your children: "There is only one of you. What does that make you? Priceless. It doesn't matter how much money you have. If there is only one of something, it is irreplaceable."

Being irreplaceable is a message your children need to know is true for them, too. They need to hear that over and over again, because the world is trying as hard as it can to devalue people. The world is aborting children, while things and possessions are treated with respect. Children are seen as a burden, while nature and animals are touted as sacred. That is why you need to prove to your children—through your words, your actions, and your life—how valuable they are. They need to be told, shown, and convinced that they are one-of-a-kind.

I use this message of value when talking about drugs, alcohol, pornography, and a number of other things. It's not just about telling them that those things are bad. It's about convincing them that their lives are of too great a value to waste on those things. I share how those things will *steal* from them. I remind them that each of us only has one chance at this life, and we shouldn't waste it. I use examples of people I know who were gifted, blessed people who let vices steal everything good from them. Vices turn people into numbers—nothing but sad statistics and examples of lost destinies. Using this approach is a lot more powerful than merely telling them it's wrong. The message is clear: *don't waste what you have been given.*

When your children understand their value, it affects how they treat and respect others. If they know they are one-of-a-kind masterpieces, then it helps them see others the same way. It helps them treat people with decency and respect. It helps them understand that people are worth fighting for—and worth sacrificing for.

The current trend of negativity and hatefulness toward one another directly stems from individuals not understanding their own value...or in return, the value of others.

Value Affects Destiny

Once children know their value, they understand a key truth about destiny. If they can't be replaced, then their destiny, which was created and given to them by God, can't be replaced either. They need to understand that only they can fulfill their destinies—no one else can do it for them. No one's destiny is the same, and theirs is as unique as they are. God put specific things in them for them to accomplish. That's why they can't waste their lives in mediocrity. The world needs their destinies to be fulfilled.

This touches on one of the unspoken tragedies of abortion. It's not only the loss of a life, but also the loss of a destiny. Forgiveness is readily available for the person who has committed the abortion; it can be covered with a single drop of Jesus's blood. But you can't replace the child, or his or her lost destiny. I sometimes wonder who we've lost to abortion...The next world leader? The doctor who would have discovered the cure for cancer? The evangelist who would have had reached millions with the gospel?

Dad, your children need to know they are not accidents. Each of them has a purpose, a destiny, a reason for existing. Convince them that they have a part to play in leaving this world a better place. Your children are valuable in this giant play called life; and not only that, but they can have an effect on eternity. What a treasure they are!

Value People Above All Else

The next value our children must learn is the value of things, possessions, and money. To be clear, I like both money and nice things. I am absolutely in favor of people being blessed with more—myself included! But you can place too great a value on things.

I've seen police rush to a house during a funeral because the children of the deceased were at the house fighting over his stuff. Were they horrible children? No, they were merely valuing what they had been taught to value.

My wife and I decided early on that we would place our value in the Lord and family *first*. We also value good friends, good relationships, and good reputations. This led us to decide that my wife wouldn't work outside the home

ASSESS YOUR CHILDREN'S VALUE

while we were raising our kids. The way I saw it, I didn't need a new car or house. I needed my wife to raise our kids to be godly men. Sure, I would love to have more money. Lord knows I could use it. I'm one of the few people who can go to McDonald's and spend $150 feeding my family! However, while money is certainly appreciated and helpful, we've made a heart decision to value relationships *more*. We still have four at home; so even though my wife has a math degree and could certainly find a job, we have decided that we get a greater return on the investment of her time when she spends it on our children.

....
Where we spend our time reveals what we value.
....

It's clear what people value by the way they live their lives. To some, sports and recreation are most important. To others, having the latest and greatest car, house, or toy is a must. For others, it's always wearing designer clothes. These are all values that the world is screaming at each of us to treasure, but we must choose to value true riches. By our own lives, our kids will learn what is—and what is not—most important.

I want my children to value the things of God, His Word, and His presence. Because of that, we go to church, we read the Bible at home, and we worship together in our house. I value them knowing God. That value drives all the parenting decisions I make.

I also want them to value each other. When we are all together, I'll often say to them, "Boys, the most important people in your lives are in this room," and, "You're going to love and support each other." I'll frequently make them go to each other's events to show that they value their brothers. As they've gotten older, I love to watch them now take care of each other. It's a priceless reward!

From Benjamin, my fifth oldest son:

> *At Family Time, Dad said two things to us more often than anything else. The first: "You boys are the greatest gift God has ever given me, and I'm proud to be your dad." The second: "Look around this room, boys. The most important people in your life are sitting in this room, and y'all are gonna love each other and be there for each other for the rest of your lives."*
>
> *It was never a question that Dad loved and valued us, and that he wanted us to love and value each other, too.*

The value of something is not based on how much it costs to create it. It's in how much people are willing to pay for it. Many items don't get manufactured because they simply aren't valuable enough for consumers to invest in them. That

ASSESS YOUR CHILDREN'S VALUE

certainly wasn't the case with God and us. He demonstrated mankind's value not at creation but at Calvary. When He paid the ultimate price by giving us His Son, Jesus Christ, He demonstrated just how valuable people are to Him. He established mankind's value the moment He showed how much He was willing to pay for us!

Dad, you have to know what's truly valuable and convince your children of it. They must first know *their* value, or they will always settle for less than they're worth. Then, they must learn to value those things that are most important—the Lord, the Word, and the people God has placed in their lives. Everything else is a distant fourth.

Key Points

1. Your children need to understand their own value. It's a key to them fulfilling their destinies and in helping them see value in others.
2. Children learn to value what their parents value. Therefore, you have a responsibility to teach your children to value what matters most: a relationship with God, His Word, and other people. All those things are more valuable than possessions, toys, or status symbols.
3. God demonstrated the importance of value—and the value of each person—when He gave His Son for the sins of mankind. This shows how valuable people are to God and should be to us.

Discussion Questions

1. What have you taught your children to value? How have you done this?
2. How do you demonstrate that you value what matters most to God in a world that values temporary things like possessions, toys, designer clothes, and status symbols? Give practical examples.

3. How do you think it will affect your children when they understand their destiny? How do you think it will affect their relationships and communication with family, friends, and strangers?

Take Action

Begin teaching your children about their value. Remind them that each of them is a one-of-a-kind masterpiece. Remind them of this as they interact with their brothers, sisters, extended family, friends, and strangers. I also strongly suggest that you have a Family Time together at the end of the day. It's a great place to remind your children of their value as individuals and to the family.

4

Understand Your Children's Destiny

"Before I formed you in the womb I knew you..."
(Jeremiah 1:5)

When did I know I was a man? Was it when I turned 18? No, I know a lot of men in their 40s who still act like children. Was it when I got my first fulltime job? Nope. I see grown people behave like spoiled 3-year-olds at work. Was it when I became a father? Sorry. I know men who never take responsibility for the children they have. Something changed in me and I became a man *when my father told me I was a man.*

Dads Give Identity

Throughout the Bible, God pronounced to people who they were long before they ever became the men they were destined to be. This was true for Gideon when God appeared to him while he was hiding in a wine press and declared, "Hail, mighty man of valor" (Judges 6:11). This was also true for David when God sent Samuel to anoint him as king of Israel even though David was a lowly shepherd at the time (see 1 Samuel 16). God didn't see them as who they were in those moments; He saw who they were meant to be, who they were destined to be. That's what a good father does.

My father used to say to me all the time, right before I walked out the door, "Remember your last name."

What was he saying? Was it a helpful hint in case I got lost on my way home? Of course not. All my life he had taught me that in this world of chaos and trouble we are *Hickmans*. That meant something. He taught me that by telling me, by showing me through his example, and by making me live a certain way.

All the time he would say, "If you are going to live here and be part of this family..." He wasn't being mean or condescending. He was simply reminding me of who I was and what I was created and trained to be.

One of my favorite books, *Turkeys and Eagles* by Peter Lord, tells the story of a baby eagle that falls out of its nest and takes up with a rafter of turkeys. The eagle lives like a turkey, blinded to the glaring fact that he's an eagle. He goes on living as a turkey until one day he finally realizes who he is. He stops settling for living as a turkey when he discovers he was an eagle all along. No longer does he settle for less than his true self, his true identity. His life changed from that moment forward.

Obviously, Peter Lord is not talking about livestock, but rather character, value, and self-worth. He's using an allegory to speak to the importance of understanding our true identity and living up to it. As a father, you have both the right and the responsibility to call out the eagle in your children, to help establish them in their identity so they can push through the confusion of the world they live in and rise above the temptations to live like a turkey.

That's one of the worst things about the theory of evolution, by the way—it's a fallacy that devalues people. I have spoken to real scientists, people without agendas, and they all say there is no way we evolved from slime. It's a scientific impossibility. But in the eyes of evolutionists, people are merely part of the animal kingdom instead of the crown jewel of a creation that was made in the likeness and image of God. People need to know they are special, priceless, and belong to something great!

The ABCs of Identity

When my wife was pregnant with our second boy, she got this wild idea to have a home birth. Personally, I don't recommend it! But, since she was the one who had to birth the child, I agreed. As you can imagine, it was a bit...stressful. The baby ended up being much bigger than expected, and he took longer to enter this world than expected.

I was a wreck. *Finally,* with the help of a midwife, the baby came—a 10-pound, 4-ounce little boy. *WOW!*

During all the stress, I didn't have much time to pray about a name. Two days later, I felt like the Lord led me to the name Caleb. I shared it with Amy, and we agreed to ask God to confirm it. The next day a lady in our church came by our house and said very reluctantly, "I felt like the Lord wanted me to tell you to name your son Caleb." Amy and I laughed out loud.

....

> As a father, it is my job to tell my children who they are. It is my job to point them in the right direction and let them fly. It is my job to show them what it is to be godly men with purpose. It is my job to show them how to treat and love a woman by the way I treat and love their mother. It is my job to give each of them an identity. I won't accomplish this in a day. It's a daily practice that I must do as their dad. It takes time, but it is time well spent.

....

That experience confirmed in me the need to convince Caleb and all his brothers that they were not accidents. God knew them by name before they were born. Jeremiah 1:5 says, "I knew you in the womb." They were supposed to be here. They are wanted and loved. God has something great for them, because God only does great things.

UNDERSTAND YOUR CHILDREN'S DESTINY

As a father, it is my job to tell my children who they are. It is my job to point them in the right direction and let them fly. It is my job to show them what it is to be godly men with purpose. It is my job to show them how to treat and love a woman by the way I treat and love their mother. It is my job to give each of them an identity. I won't accomplish this in a day. It's a daily practice that I must do as their dad. It takes time, but it is time well spent.

With this in mind, you can see why our country is in crisis—specifically, an *identity* crisis. We have no sense of right and wrong, no sense of purpose, and are groping in the dark for some semblance of identity. People look at their physical bodies and wonder if they're male or female. I believe this confusion all stems from the effects of raising a fatherless generation. People are trying to find themselves; but that's an impossible task without a father, because identity comes from a father. *Fathers are irreplaceable!*

When God said, "This is my beloved Son in whom I am well pleased," it was not because of Jesus's performance. At that time, Jesus hadn't performed a single miracle. He said it because of who Jesus was. The power of that identity carried Jesus through every circumstance of life. It gave Him the platform from which to fulfill His destiny. It was that revelation that kept Him during temptation and led Him to victory.

Dad, over and over again your children need to hear words like: "I love you...I'm proud of you...You're mine!" "You're a good son (daughter), and you're gonna be a great man (woman)." "From the time you were born, I knew God had great plans for your life." You have to convince them that they belong to something bigger than themselves. Identity starts with words, something we'll cover in more depth in chapter 8.

Many parents fall into the trap of praising their children only when they've performed well and criticizing them whenever they perform poorly. This causes them to assume that their identity and your love for them are tied to their performance, neither of which should be true. You must avoid this trap. If you only share your love with them when they do something good, they will intuitively assume that their worth and identity is based on their performance. Praise them and love them because of who they are, *your son or your daughter*. They belong to *you*. They make you proud, completely aside from their performance. I have told my boys that since before they could speak.

Proverbs 18:20-21 says that your words have power. I don't want my children to ever wonder whether their dad loves them. I don't want them to ever question whether I am for them; so, I constantly remind them how I feel about them and who they are.

UNDERSTAND YOUR CHILDREN'S DESTINY

They can rely on that. Even when they mess up and I have to discipline them, they know I love them. They may not like the correction, but they know they never have to question my love for them. They're my sons, and they are accepted because of that fact. Period.

Affirming your children doesn't mean you're okay with every one of their actions. There will certainly be times when you'll have to correct specific behaviors, especially those relating to effort and character. We'll discuss discipline in more detail in future chapters. For now, understand that you want to correct from a foundation of identity: "You're my son, and I know you're better than that. I love you too much to allow you to behave that way."

To give you a better idea of what I'm talking about, I want to give you my ABCs of identity along with examples of what you would say when addressing each area:

- **Ability:** *"You can do it."*
  Give your children your vote of confidence. Help them believe they can succeed.
- **Belonging:** *"Even if you never win a game, I'll always be proud to be your dad."*
  Let your children know that they have a place to come back to regardless of how they perform.
- **Character:** *"We're (insert your last name)s. We don't quit!"*

Instill important characteristics that will follow your children to every sport they play and every job they take.

Like Gideon, David, and Jesus, you must call out the good in your children before you ever see it, beginning at a very young age. You're seeing the good in them and calling it out rather than solely treating them according to where they may be at the time. If you wait for your children to become good men or women before you ever call them that, they may never get there.

God Called You His Own

Dad, if you don't know who you are because your father never told you, God the Father will be happy to tell you and give you the identity you need. He loves to speak His love to us! I remember one time when I was preaching at a church and the Lord had me look at this large, elderly gentleman. He was an intimidating man, standing very tall. He looked like a hard-working farmer.

The Lord told me to tell him, "God the Father is your Father, and He loves you and is so proud of you." This giant man walked straight up to me and fell on my shoulder and began to weep.

"I have always wondered whether I really belong," he said. "My earthly dad never said he was proud of me or loved me. I have always wondered who I am. Today, the love of the Father set me free."

Dad, you have the ability to give your children the very foundation of life—their identity. Don't waste it. Don't neglect it. Don't leave your children searching for it. Their futures depend on it.

Key Points

1. Fathers give their children identity. You give your children identity when you, as their father, tell them you love them and are proud of them often and repeatedly, without tying it to their performance.
2. Without identity, people will be left confused about who they are, what their purpose is, and what their worth is. Identity is built daily, but not in a day. Build your children's identity daily through encouraging words, unconditional love and support, and by reaffirming their character.

Discussion Questions

1. When did you know you were a man?
2. How do you think a lack of identity will affect your children's lives?
3. Why is it important to give your children identity apart from performance?
4. How can you give your children identity? Give practical ways.
5. What is your identity? Did your father give identity to you? If not, how have you received your identity from your heavenly Father?

Take Action

Think of the identity you want to give to your children. What ways can you do this for each child? Take note of any changes you see in your children as a result of sharing their identity with them.

5

Build a Secure Foundation

*And a voice from heaven said, "This is my Son,
whom I love; with him I am well pleased."*
(Matthew 3:17)

There was a time that Amy and I found ourselves with seven boys under the age of 10. Needless to say, those were exciting times.

One of our favorite games was "RAH!" We would turn off all the lights in the house except for one candle in the living room where Amy and the baby would sit. All the other boys would wait around the candle while I hid somewhere in the house. After building up some anticipation, the boys would have to come and find me. The catch was that the boys had to remain together wherever they went. I would hide on top of dressers, on countertops, in the back of closets, or lying in a bathtub. (I'll still be here when you're done laughing at the picture of my big self climbing on furniture!)

The boys would hold hands and walk slowly through each room in our dark house, hunting for me. When they entered the room where I was hiding, I would wait until all of them got inside and then jump up from my hiding spot and scream, "RAHHHHH!!!!!"

Immediate panic ensued! They'd run into each other, crash into walls, and scream bloody murder trying to get away. They would run over furniture, each other, and anything else that got in the way. Their sole goal was to get safely back to the candle with Mom.

Sometimes one or two of them would scream and run into things until they realized it was me. Then they'd scream while running *toward* me—because they knew *Dad loves me. Dad is for me. I don't know what's happening, but I'm better with Dad around.* They would run to me with hands lifted high. I'd pick them up, and we would walk to the light and all sit around laughing until it was time to go again.

....

You have the ability and calling to give your children security. I believe that Jesus walked this earth because of the security He had in the love of His Father.

....

Dad, you have the ability and calling to give your children security. I believe that Jesus walked this earth because of the security He had in the love of His Father.

Throughout the Bible, Scripture gives us clues that Jesus knew who He was and understood His value. He knew that the Father's love for Him was a settled fact.

How did the Father give that kind of security to Jesus, and how can we as fathers give it to our children? Here are some keys to doing that.

Promote Security Apart from Performance

Throughout Jesus's life, He didn't have the pressure to perform. Looking once more at Jesus's baptism in Matthew 3, God's voice came from heaven saying, "This is my beloved Son, in whom I am well pleased" (v. 17 NKJV). God violated the natural laws of creation and let His audible voice be heard to declare His pleasure in His Son.

You might say, "Well, if Jesus was my son, I'd certainly be proud of Him, too. Look at all He did."

But remember, up to that point Jesus hadn't done anything extraordinary: no miracles, no signs, and no great feats. God said He loved Jesus simply because Jesus was His Son. What a good dad!

All too often I see parents at sports or other events who only express their love for their children when they do well. When the children do poorly, the parents get angry. As a result, I see children *and* adults walking around insecure because of the effects of this type of parenting.

Insecurity is a cancer to the soul. It eats away at a person's confidence, dreams, and the ability to believe and act on those beliefs. Insecurity steals the joy of living. When someone's insecure, he can never really feel love because he can't believe anyone would love him. Insecurity also opens the door to fear and all sorts of emotions like anger and jealousy.

I watch so many people live their whole lives without ever knowing the security of who they are, never understanding their own value or the peace that security brings. They settle for less because of it.

Dad, you have the opportunity and anointing to give your children security, to know they are loved and valued *no matter what*. It's something you must convince them of, and it's something you're equipped to do.

Follow the Father's Heart

Luke 15 tells the story of the prodigal son. In it, a child decides to take his inheritance early and leave his father behind. The son proceeds to waste all he has on wild living. It cost him dearly. And, when he ran out of money and a severe drought struck the land, the son found himself eating from the same trough with pigs to survive. That's when he knew he had hit rock bottom. Eventually, he worked up the courage to return home to his father. What an incredible passage every father should read! Think about it—what made the son want to return home?

If home hadn't been a secure place, he never would have gone back. I believe he knew his dad was going to welcome him back, even after all the things he had done wrong.

I remember the one and only time I was arrested and taken to jail. I didn't understand why there was a warrant out for my arrest. I didn't understand what was happening, but I knew what I needed to do...call Dad. Turns out, I had an unpaid ticket. In the midst of confusion and trouble, all I could think of was, *Just get Dad here.* My earthly father had made me secure in his love—a truly powerful gift.

Dad, you must do two things to make your children feel secure: establish order in your household, and make it clear that you are for them, not against them.

Establish Order in Your Household

First, you must establish the proper order in your household. This doesn't start with your children, but with your wife. Getting your priorities straight is so important. If you ask my boys where they rank in my heart, they will tell you that they are a strong third.

- *The Lord is first.*
- *Their mother is second.*
- *My boys are third.*

Understanding this order gives them security. I love the Lord *first*, so they have security in knowing that I'm striving to live a godly life. I'm not going to mistreat them or their mother, and they know I'm going to be the same man no matter where I am. This makes them secure.

> ...one of the best things you can do for your kids as a father is to love their mother well.

Some dads might have a hard time with this and think that the kids should be more important than the parents. However, one of the best things you can do for your kids as a father is to love their mother well. It will benefit both them and you. Not only was she there before them, she'll be there after they're gone.

If the marriage isn't prioritized, things can fall apart, causing harm to the parents and the children. Studies show that kids can actually experience trauma from witnessing their parents fight in front of them. You're not hurting them by valuing their mother most. You're keeping their world stable and secure.

From Jacob, my third oldest son:

> *Growing up, the quickest way to get Dad into full-on disciplinarian mode was to talk back to Mom. My mom is a small woman, no more than 4'11", yet she has 11 boys.*

> *Dad would never let us disrespect her; and if we did, it always brought about what he jokingly called "sudden and swift retribution."*
>
> *I remember when my mom was homeschooling five of us at the same time in five different grades—and she had an infant. We respected and listened to this little woman (for the most part:) because we knew that if we didn't she would call Dad from work, and he would always back her up.*
>
> *One of Dad's favorite jokes to tell us was, "Me and Amy brought you into this world, and we can take you out... and make another one just like you." For a guy who had 11 sons, you kind of believed him. Ultimately, I didn't ever feel jealous that my dad loved my mom like that. I was glad. It made me feel safe, like I never had to worry about anything happening to them.*

Make It Clear that You Are For Them

Secondly, once they are secure in their position in your household, you must demonstrate to them that you are *for* them, that you have their best interests at heart. Your children have to be convinced of this. They have to know that nothing they do will ever change your love for them. Convincing them of this takes a lot of time, effort, and action: but it's necessary both when they do right and when they do wrong, because the same heart blesses and disciplines.

We're not supposed to use our children to relive our youth or find some sense of pride to make us feel better. Our job is to create an atmosphere where our kids can discover their destinies and go for it. We're to build a platform that helps them jump into life. They have to be secure to do that, or they won't jump very far...or possibly not at all.

Being for them also includes helping them know that you are willing to fight and sacrifice for their well-being. Most of us don't have to physically fight to demonstrate this, but if you are going to live a fulfilled life, you are going to have to fight for them emotionally and spiritually by being an involved, Spirit-led father.

For me, this didn't involve physical fights, but it certainly involved personal sacrifices. There was a time when I played golf...a lot. I was good at it, and I loved to play. As I began having children, I realized that if I continued to play as much as I was, it would get in the way of spending time with my kids and them spending time with me. I could keep the title of being a good golfer, but I would lose the chance to be a great dad. As a result, I gave up playing so much and began investing that time into teaching them to play and being with them for other things.

Don't get me wrong—I'm not a perfect dad, but I am willing to fight and sacrifice for my boys. Not only do *I* know this is true, but my boys know it's true, too. They are convinced my wife and I will fight for their successes and even sacrifice to make those successes possible.

Discovering that results in personal security, and it's something you need to instill in your children. You won't accomplish this with a one-time statement or action. No, you have to prove it every day by your words and actions.

Helping your children become secure will allow them to go for their destinies. It's a different model from today's common practices. Modern wisdom says that we must create safe spaces where children never face difficulty or experience pain or hardship. That's not a realistic goal; quite frankly, it's a damaging one. Security isn't about giving children a place to hide or protecting them so that they never do anything hard or risky. Instead, security is about building a strength within them so they can withstand external pressures and hardship. It's about helping them be brave enough to go for their destinies even though it's hard.

A sense of security serves as a foundation for your children to fulfill the calling God has on each one of their lives—to be good, godly men and women, full of character, who understand they are called to make their world better.

There is a shortage of men and women like this in our culture and our world. Wherever their destiny takes them, I want my children to make this world a better place, and

I encourage you to help yours do the same. Let's fight and sacrifice, so that they become those kinds of people.

Dad, providing security to your children is not a one-time choice. It's not a one-time statement. It's not a one-time action. It's a daily, weekly, say it/live it over and over again part of your life. Your children need to be told *constantly* that you are for them, because the world is constantly screaming that they are alone, worthless, and unloved. Prove to them that the world is wrong.

Key Points

1. Children need to know they are loved and valued regardless of their performance.
2. A sense of security allows children—and eventually adults—to pursue their dreams and callings, to accept that they are loved, and to experience joy in life.
3. Your children will become secure when there is order (right priority given to the relationships) in the home, and when they know that you are for them and will fight and sacrifice for them.

Discussion Questions

1. When did God express His love for Jesus? Was it before or after Jesus began His ministry on earth? Why is this an important model for all fathers?
2. How can you instill a sense of security in your children?
3. Did you experience a sense of security or a lack of security from your own father? How did this affect you?
4. Why do you think a sense of security is so important to your children? How do you think it will affect them later in life?

5. How do your priorities affect your children's sense of security? What can you do in your home that would provide a sense of order for your children?
6. Do you agree that instilling a sense of security in your children will be an ongoing process and not a one-time event? What can you do to keep that process consistent?

Take Action

Begin expressing your love and admiration for your children apart from their performance. Let them know you are for them and invested in their success—not for your own fulfillment, but for their well-being.

SECTION 2
LET'S TALK
ABOUT LOVE

"Thou shalt love..." That's the command Jesus gave in Matthew 22:37 when a Pharisee asked Him to name the most important commandment. In that moment, He wanted mankind to understand the significance of love—how to love our heavenly Father and how to love one another.

To find out what real love looks like, read 1 Corinthians 13. That passage begins with, "Love is," and lists love's many characteristics. This is important to your role as a father because children must be *convinced* that they are loved with a 1 Corinthians 13 kind of love.

Understand, love is not an emotion or feeling. It is a choice. That's an important distinction. My emotions and feelings can be fickle. Sometimes my children are not very lovable. For these reasons, my feelings and emotions must be subject to my choices. There are times when I don't feel like correcting or disciplining or playing with my children, but I *choose* to do those things—and more—because of love.

Love is the choice you make every day that gives you the strength to raise godly children in this crazy world.

This section is about the process and the different ways the Lord has shown me to love my boys. It's not an all-inclusive list, but specific strategies that help convince children they are loved, methods I know work—and work well. Then, from that platform of love and security, we can prepare our children to conquer their worlds.

6

Let Them Know They're Special

"Indeed, the very hairs of your head are all numbered. Don't be afraid; you are worth more than many sparrows."
(Luke 12:7)

Hundreds of years ago, there was a village in a small province in China that was known all over the world for its urns. The whole village took part in creating them. Some villagers crafted the urns, some sanded them, and some skillfully painted them. When each urn was complete, the village would gather around and drop the urn to *break* it. Then, they would gather every little piece and reassemble the urn using gold-infused glue.

Because they broke differently, each urn went from a beautiful utilitarian jar to a one-of-a-kind masterpiece. It was impossible to recreate or replace the uniqueness of a fully finished urn, making each one priceless.

Psalm 139 says that we are "fearfully and wonderfully made." Each of us was made in the image of God. We are all one-of-a-kind masterpieces, made to fellowship with God. This is also true of your children. God was there in the beginning, infusing their DNA with gifts, talents, likes, dislikes, qualities, and attributes. All those things make them special, one-of-a-kind masterpieces. Just look at the fingerprints of God's children—each one is unique.

Your job as a father is to make every one of your children feel special. You need them to feel celebrated and irreplaceable. Here are a few techniques that I've found work well and have instilled a sense of importance in my children.

Pay Attention

The first way you can help your children believe they are as special as God says they are is by giving them the attention they need. You need to look them in the eye and listen to them. You need to pay attention to what is going on around them and in their lives.

Satan is constantly trying to destroy your children, steal their destiny, and rob them of any good blessings God wants to give them. It is your job to be aware of this, protect them, and stand in the gap for them.

When boys or girls hit 12 or 13, they go through something I still don't have the words to describe. (I sometimes think they should be locked up until they are 16 or 17!) During that time, they are battling between childhood and adulthood. That's when they begin to listen to other voices besides yours. You have to be all up in their business to know what's going on. Don't be lazy and say, "Aww, that's just kids. They'll grow out of it." Don't let them isolate themselves from you. Don't let them spend hours in their room with a computer, video games, or their phone. No, get into their world.

To know what is going on, you must pay attention. To pay attention, you must be involved in what they do and care about.

Create Family Time at Meals

Even though we have a big family, one of the best ways we made everyone feel special was by talking during our family dinners. No phones, no TV, just talk. I would ask each child how his day was and what the best thing about it was. I made the other boys listen to each other because it made the one speaking feel special when he was heard. It also gave me a chance to hear each one's heart, so I would pay close attention to what they said and how they said it. It takes time to do this, but not as much as you think. And it's well worth the investment.

From Caleb, my second oldest son:

> *At times, it was hectic growing up in a family of 13. That's 13 different people with 13 different schedules and each with varying priorities. However, no matter how much or how little was going on in a week, we always made time for family each day. The sole driving force behind that was—and still is—my father.*

> *He made it a priority for us to spend time together. This more often than not consisted of a family meal each night. We would all sit around the table and have dinner together and share the high and low points of our day. (Mother is a great cook, by-the-way.)*
>
> *It didn't matter if a friend or other people were at the house. Dad would have them pull up a chair and participate like they were part of our family. Making this a priority and a habit allowed each of us to grow comfortable with each other and respect each other's opinions. Most importantly, spending daily, quality time with each other inevitably caused each person to love every other person. To this day, when one of us is not at the table, he is missed.*
>
> *The family is not complete without each and every person in the room.*

Make Birthdays Special

Another way we tried to make our boys feel special was on their birthdays. We learned this from the Bible. The angels showed up to celebrate Jesus's birthday. It also says that the angels throw a party and celebrate a person's spiritual birthday, the day they come to know Christ. I figure if they do it, so can we.

Family birthdays that make children feel special don't have to cost a lot of money. Some people go way overboard, but that's not what makes it special to the child. It's the little things that make them feel special: having a special plate to eat their meals on, eating their favorite breakfast, playing their favorite game while everybody participates. All these things are cheap, fun, and effective. Children can't help but feel special when their family gathers around them to celebrate the day they were born.

> If your children are going to believe they are special, you're going to have to affirm it in them with your words.

Repeat These Words, Over and Over

We will talk about the power of words in greater detail in chapter 8; but for now, understand that children feel special through the words their parents speak to them. Your children need you to look them in the eyes and hear you say, "I love you so much." They need to hear it over and over again. They need to hear you tell fond stories of them growing up. They need to hear how excited you were when they were born. They need to hear you say how proud you are to be their dad. If your children are going to believe they are special, you're going to have to affirm it in them with your words.

All the science that has to happen for a child to be born reaffirms my belief in a Creator and the uniqueness of each life. Children should be treated with this in mind, especially by their dads. Fathers play a unique role in making their children feel and know that that they are special. Never underestimate the important role you play in them fulfilling their destinies and accepting the blessings God has for them.

Key Points

1. Fathers help their children believe that they are "knit together in their mother's womb," a one-of-a-kind masterpiece that cannot be replaced.
2. Your children need to know that they are special. This knowledge prepares them to fulfill their destiny and accept the blessings God has for them.
3. In order to know your children, you must pay attention. This means getting involved in your children's lives, what they care about and do.

Discussion Questions

1. Why do you think it is important for your children to view themselves as masterpieces?
2. Do you believe that your paying attention to your children will make a difference in their lives? If so, how can you pay more attention to them?
3. What are some ways that you can get to know your children? Include ways that are not discussed in this chapter.

Take Action

List three things you can do to make your children feel special, and then write them into your schedule. Ideas include family breakfasts or dinners, birthday celebrations, words of affirmation, etc.

1. _____
   _____
   _____

2. _____
   _____
   _____

3. _____
   _____
   _____

7

Love Is Spelled T-I-M-E

*For I am persuaded, that neither death nor life,
nor angels nor principalities nor powers, nor things present
nor things to come, nor height nor depth, nor any other
created thing, shall be able to separate us from the love of
God, which is in Christ Jesus our Lord.*
(Romans 8:38-39)

Nerf wars were a great source of fun when my sons were younger. We'd tear around the house shooting each other, laughing the whole time. When poor Mom would walk in the room, we'd all turn our guns on her. She'd scream, and we'd collapse in laughter. (Disclaimer: No moms were ever hurt in the Hickman family Nerf wars...for the most part.) To this day, we still laugh and reminisce about those wars. Other than buying Nerf guns for our boys on their birthdays or Christmas, it was an inexpensive pastime. The only thing it required was *time*.

Time is the great equalizer. Man or woman, rich or poor, no matter their location on this earth, every person has the same number of hours in his or her day. As I mentioned in chapter 3, where we spend our time clearly shows what we value most. And just as our children learn what is and isn't important by what we model, they also learn whether we value *them* by whether we make time for them in our busy schedules. For children, love is often spelled T-I-M-E.

....

Dad, you want to *be there* for those moments.
You want to *remember* those moments.
And even more, you want to be the *reason*
for those moments.

....

Playtime is Never Wasted

One of the best ways to say "I love you" is to play with your kids. That's good news because, like those Nerf wars, quality time doesn't require a lot of money or large pieces of equipment. It simply requires that you make space in your schedule.

Thankfully, the payoff is well worth it. There's nothing quite like hearing your children laugh and seeing smiles that can't be hidden flash across their faces. It's priceless! Dad, you want to *be there* for those moments. You want to *remember* those moments. And even more, you want to be the *reason* for those moments.

LOVE IS SPELLED T-I-M-E

As I mentioned at the beginning of this book, I chose to teach my boys to play golf when they were young with the hope of us being able to play golf together for the rest of our lives. To this day, we enjoy heading out to the course for a few rounds. It's nothing short of awesome, and one of the best visions I set early on and followed through with. It's never been about winning and losing. It's about enjoying time together in the beautiful outdoors.

Golf is one way we like to spend time together, but you may have something else you choose to do with your children. You may love throwing a ball in the yard, or camping, gardening, doing woodwork, or working on cars. You may prefer playing board games or building models or LEGO blocks. The goal is to spend time with your children, pure and simple.

Let me stop here to correct a misconception. Taking your kids to ball practice, dance class, or karate is NOT spending time with them, even if you coach. There is nothing wrong with those things, but it doesn't count as time spent one-on-one with you. You are irreplaceable in your children's lives. They need to go for walks and drives with you. They need to laugh and cry with you. They need to see you do life and model it in front of them, so they know how to live their own lives. That takes time—personal, by your side, one-on-one time.

I also caution you not to fill your children's schedules with too many activities so that their time is unavailable for you.

Don't think that by limiting those activities you are withholding something good from them. Instead, realize that you are freeing them up to spend time with the most important person in their lives—their dad.

My wife and I allowed our boys to participate in one activity each semester. That was all. We didn't want all their energy, attention, and time spent elsewhere. We wanted them to have space in their schedules for home, family, and especially for time with dad. They were still able to pursue sports and activities. A few of them have even gone on to play at the college level. And not one of them has ever come home and complained that he spent too much time with me when he was young. Quite the contrary. Spending time with me helped lay a foundation on which they could thrive in their chosen pursuits. The same is true for you and your children.

> Ask your children questions and listen to their answers. It will be well worth it.

Listen and Learn

Listening is an important part of spending time with your children. I often hear parents of teenagers say, "My children won't talk to me." Sadly, they've almost waited too long.

LOVE IS SPELLED T-I-M-E

Don't wait until your children are teenagers to communicate with them. You have to start listening to them early, laying a foundation of open communication.

How do you do this? Ask your children questions and listen to their answers. It will be well worth it. When they become teenagers and their minds are bombarded with bad thoughts and ideas, they'll still be talking to you. When that time comes, they'll let you in to their thought processes; and even though it's scary to hear what they're dealing with, you'll have the chance to speak life to them.

This is serious business. Listening to your children can be a life and death issue. Every suicide note I have ever read said the same thing: "You'll be better off without me." What a lie! If you have good communication with your children, then you have the opportunity to address those thoughts before they reach crisis mode.

As mentioned in the last chapter, my wife and I ask each of our children what they are thankful for during Family Time, and we make sure everyone is listening. Why? We want each of our boys to know he has been heard and his thoughts are important to our family.

Every one of my boys is different. They may look alike, but they all have different gifts. Each brings a unique facet to our family, and we would not be the same without each and every one of them. The same is true for your children.

By listening to them, you're reinforcing that truth. You're making it clear to them that they are heard and valued.

But again, this takes effort. It means putting away smartphones. It means not hiding in an office, workshop, or garage. It means asking questions and listening to the answers. And it all takes time—your time.

From Elisha, my eighth oldest son:

> *Our family could fill this book with stories of my brothers' crazy adventures, and times when my dad had to step in and be the disciplinary force. (I was a saint, of course.) But when I think of my dad, three practices come to mind:*
>
> 1. *If he was going to discipline one of us, he always spent just as much time building us up as he did disciplining us.*
> 2. *He never held back or was too "manly" to say how proud he was or how much he loved us.*
> 3. *He showed us how much he loved us by spending time with us.*
>
> *No amount of money can buy, and no gift can replace, the meaning and power that comes from a son hearing his father say the words "I love you" or "I'm proud of you." I've experienced this firsthand. My dad has never been too prideful or too reserved to let us know that he loves us. And he always backed those words with his actions.*

LOVE IS SPELLED T-I-M-E

> *He did not miss baseball, football, or basketball games. He spent time out in the yard playing with us or on the back porch talking about life. To a kid, T-I-M-E is how you spell LOVE. My dad always did an amazing job of not only telling us how proud he was of us and how much he loved us, but also by showing it to us by the amount of time we spent together.*

The verse I shared at the top of this chapter is this: "For I am persuaded that neither death nor life, nor angels nor principalities nor powers, nor things present nor things to come, nor height nor depth, nor any other created thing, shall be able to separate us from the love of God which is in Christ Jesus our Lord" (Romans 8:38-39 NKJV*).*

The word "persuaded" means *I can count on that.* Can you feel the strength and security in that verse? Your heavenly Father's love is unshakeable! That's the same security you want your children to have in your love. You want them to know that they can always count on your love and support because they are valuable to you. That kind of relationship doesn't happen by chance. It takes a vision, and it takes time. Don't waste the time you have with your children. Invest it wisely. Remember, there are no do-overs.

Key Points

1. Your children learn what is and isn't important by what you model. They also learn whether you value them by whether you make time for them.
2. Playing with your children is one of the best ways to communicate that you love them.
3. Listening is an important part of spending time with your children. This process can begin simply by asking questions and listening to their responses.
4. Laying a foundation of communication when your children are young makes it easier to combat bad thoughts and ideas that come to them as teenagers.

Discussion Questions

1. Why is it so important to spend time with your children? What does it communicate to them when you don't make time for them?
2. Why is listening to your children important? What does it communicate to them?
3. Why is it important to listen to your children while they are still young? How does this pay off later?
4. What is your greatest difficulty in spending time with your children?

5. What are your favorite ways to spend time with your children?

Take Action

Take time to ask questions and listen to your children this week. Not sure what to talk about? Ask them what they are thankful for. Ask them to name the best part of their day or the worst part of their day. If you ask during Family Time or over dinner, make sure the whole family listens and participates. You can even take them with you to help with a work project or home chore.

8

Create Life Through Your Words

*A man's stomach shall be satisfied from
the fruit of his mouth; from the produce of his lips he
shall be filled. Death and life are in the power of
the tongue, and those who love it will eat its fruit.*
(Proverbs 18:20-21 NKJV)

When are we going to learn just how powerful words are? Scripture tells us that life and death are in the tongue, but we can look at creation itself and see the effects of words. God *created* the world with His words. He spoke it into existence and brought forth life. You and I were created in the image of God; therefore, our words have the power to create, too. No, we won't create a physical world from nothing, but our words will either strengthen or shatter the worlds of our children.

Many people have experienced pain and devastation because of words that were spoken—or not spoken—to them by their fathers. I have ministered to hundreds of older adults and told them what their heavenly Father wanted me to say: "He loves you, and He's proud of you." The reaction that follows never ceases to amaze me. Remember the elderly man I mentioned in chapter 4 who fell on my shoulder weeping when I told him he was loved? He hadn't suffered from cruel words. He had suffered from a lack of words, leading to a lack of identity, and his anger had grown uncontrollable by the day. When he finally heard God loved him, he completely broke. Love truly conquers all.

Speak the Right Words at the Right Time

Allow me to point back once again to the words God spoke over Jesus when He said, "This is My beloved Son, in whom I am well pleased" (Matthew 3:17 NKJV).

> The Father and Jesus's relationship was important to Jesus's future and mankind's redemption. There was coming a time when the Father would ask Jesus to endure the pain and humiliation of the cross, when He would say, "No, Son. Calvary is the only way." That would require trust, respect, and obedience on Jesus's part to follow through with His Father's plan. That could only come from a healthy father-son relationship.

This moment in history was so rich because it's a picture of how we, as dads, should interact with our kids. I've already shown you how God conveyed Jesus's value and identity in that moment; but He also did something else—He affirmed His Son. Before Jesus had in any way "earned" God's favor, His Father—our heavenly Father—proclaimed to the world that He was proud of His Son. This wasn't the only time the Father announced His love for His Son, but it was the first time that humanity was privy to it.

The Father and Jesus's relationship was important to Jesus's future and mankind's redemption. There was coming a time when the Father would ask Jesus to endure the pain and humiliation of the cross, when He would say, "No, Son. Calvary is the only way." That would require trust, respect, and obedience on Jesus's part to follow through with His Father's plan. That could only come from a healthy father-son relationship.

Of course, you know the end of the story. Jesus willingly went to the cross. First John 3:16 tells us He "laid down his life for us" out of love. He heard the Father's will, trusted the Father's will, and suffered the cross in order to fulfill the Father's will. His relationship with His Father was key to humanity's redemption. Should we expect our relationships with our children to be any less trustworthy and secure?

Some may say, "But I'm not God or Jesus, and my relationship with my children won't affect humanity." I disagree. Your relationship with your children will affect your family's future—for *generations*. Your children, your grandchildren, your great-grandchildren, and your great-great-grandchildren will benefit from the healthy relationship that you establish today. Yes, there are many components to that relationship, but words are paramount.

Words can build up or tear down. They can bring healing or despair. They can set a heart at ease or a world at war. Your children not only need to hear your words, but they need to hear the *right* words at the *right* time.

Obey the 90-10 Rule

One of the most successful communication strategies for fathers is the 90-10 rule: ninety-percent of a dad's words should be positive and kind, and only 10% should be correction. Children need to be built up. You want to praise them, tell them how wonderful they are, how proud you are of them, and how much you love them. They need to hear those words over and over again. It builds their souls and gives them a foundation of love. Remember, you are building who they are by establishing their value and identity. As I've mentioned, this process isn't a one-time event. It's a constant process.

It's important to note that you shouldn't only say positive things when your children do something good. Whether it's sports, dance, school, or anything else, if you only praise them when they do well, they will learn that your love is

CREATE LIFE THROUGH YOUR WORDS

based on their performance. That will create one of two outcomes. It'll either make them extremely insecure or extremely prideful. Both are detrimental.

From Micah, my oldest son:

> *My dad has not only led by example, but he has also taught by example. He has lived his lessons daily in front of my brothers and me. Yes, he has spent money on us, but more importantly he has spent—and continues to spend—his time, his effort, and his words on us! The power of his words carries more weight to me than any other human's words ever. Though there are other mentors in my life who speak into my career and interests, my dad's words and approval tower over them all.*
>
> *I have a wife and two children now, with a third on the way. My life has grown beyond my dad's wings. Yet still, words can't explain how I feel when my dad looks me in the eyes, calls me by name, and says, "Son, you're a good man, a great husband, and an amazing father. I'm so proud of you." Those are such simple sentences, but the value and weight of those words are without compare!*
>
> *Hearing my dad's approval—the best dad I know—can't be quantified. My dad's example and its effect on me has taught me a valuable parenting lesson: my children must hear my love and approval of them on a constant basis, regardless of their accomplishments or shortcomings.*

Speak Words that Affirm

Your words need to build your children up in a world that is tearing them down. Other kids are cruel. There will always be bullying and kids throwing around hurtful words, so, at home, you want to spend a significant amount of time building them up.

Remember, 10% of your words need to correct. We'll cover discipline in upcoming chapters, but understand that correction involves telling them, "You made a bad choice." Notice that statement doesn't say *they* were bad. You never want to call your children "bad". Their choices may have been bad, but *they* never are.

Often men err on one of two sides. They either get angry and allow their words to become weapons that wound their children's souls, or their words are too sparse. They only point out what is wrong or don't say anything at all. Either of these approaches is damaging.

The Bible says that it is by the mouth of the righteous a city is exalted (see Proverbs 11:11). If our words can affect a city, then they can certainly affect our children. Let your words build up your children so that they can, in turn, build something great and affect this world for God's glory.

Key Points

1. God used words to create the universe. Since we're made in His image, our words are important, too.
2. God's affirmation of Jesus helped prepare Jesus for the cross.
3. Ninety-percent of your words to your children should be positive and kind. Only 10% should be correction.
4. You need to counteract the negativity of this world that is trying to tear your children down.

Discussion Questions

1. How did God's words of affirmation for Jesus affect Jesus's endurance of Calvary?
2. How could your lack of words (or silence) toward your children be just as detrimental and harsh as attacking words?
3. What words did you hear from your own father that still affect you today? How does this affect your parenting?
4. What is the 90-10 rule? How can you enact this rule in the words that you speak with your children?
5. How could your positive, affirming words to your children counteract the words of the world?

Take Action

List three positive things you want your children to know. Do you want them to know how proud you are of them, how much you love them, which qualities you respect in them, how much better your life is because God gave them to you? Share these positive points with your children this week. Then commit to make verbal affirmations to your children a daily habit.

1. _____
   _____
   _____

2. _____
   _____
   _____

3. _____
   _____
   _____

9

The What and Why of Discipline

Correct your son, and he will give you rest;
yes, he will give delight to your soul.
(Proverbs 29:17 NKJV)

We live in a time when many children are out of control. Parents are quick to blame their children's actions and attitudes on television, schools, video games, and anything other than themselves. Sadly, they've forgotten a key component to their parenting: *discipline*.

It's easy to lose sight of the fact that God didn't give your children to the school system, the government, or anybody else. He gave them to *you*. That means they're your responsibility. If they behave in a way that you don't approve of, it's not the school's job to correct them; it's yours.

You must discipline your children. It's not a matter of *if*, but of *when* and *how*. Your little angels—those apples of your eye—come ready-made to sin. You don't have to teach them to lie, have bad attitudes, or throw fits. It's just in them, part of the sin nature born into every one of us.

Drive Out Foolishness

Proverbs 22:15 (KJV) says, "Foolishness *is* bound in the heart of a child; *but* the rod of correction will drive it far from him."

Foolishness is simply in each of our children from the moment they are born. As their father, it's *your* responsibility to drive out the foolishness that exists in your children's hearts.

When I talk about the "rod of correction" sometimes I start to lose some people. Don't let that be you. The Bible is very clear that we must have a rod of correction. This rod isn't about abuse; of course, I would never advocate such a thing. Yes, I believe in spanking, but spanking and abuse are two entirely different things. We'll dive deeper into this in chapter 10, but for now, suffice it to say that spanking, and all other healthy forms of discipline, are correction that comes from a place of love. Abuse leads to long-term pain and comes from a place of anger, humiliation, and loss of control, none of which are reflected in God's kingdom.

As a pastor, I've seen up close the devastation and heartache that abuse causes. Thankfully, we have a Savior and a Comforter—Jesus and the Holy Spirit—who are big enough to help us heal from painful childhoods. Because of the total healing that they provide, I'm certain you can learn to discipline your own children in a way that brings joy, not shame

THE WHAT AND WHY OF DISCIPLINE

(see Proverbs 29:15), to you as a parent and to them as future men and women of God.

Discipline is Love

Many parents struggle with the nagging sense that discipline is unloving; nothing could be further from the truth. Discipline *is* love.

Let me say that again: *discipline is love.*

You may have never thought of it that way, but when you do, you'll see your responsibilities as a father in a whole new light.

God the Father says in His Word, "He who withholds the rod [of discipline] hates his son, but he who loves him disciplines and trains him diligently and appropriately [with wisdom and love]" (Proverbs 13:24 AMP).

Those are powerful words.

Every child comes with enormous potential for both good or bad, but because we live in a sinful world, there's a natural pull for children, if left to themselves, to gravitate toward the *bad.* And that's precisely why we can't leave them alone to find their own ways through life.

If you've ever planted a garden, you know what it means to tend it. You can't simply plant the seed, walk away, and expect to come back to a thriving harvest. You have to *cultivate the soil* to ensure that weeds don't choke out what you've sown. You have to get rid of the predators and insects that would attack the fruit. If you don't, what began as something beautiful and promising can quickly turn into an overwhelming problem.

The same is true for parenting. If I love my children, I'll take the time to pull the weeds—poor behaviors and attitudes—that I see forming in the fertile soil of their lives. I'll also keep away predators—the bad influences begging for their attention—to the best of my ability.

Hebrews 12:6 says, "For whom the LORD loves He chastens, and scourges every son whom He receives." If the Lord disciplines you and me because He loves us, how could we expect to do anything different with our children?

Allowing your children to throw fits, yell at their mother or any authority figure, and pout and whine until they get their way is *not* a sign of love. If you allow that type of behavior, you are essentially cursing your children with a lifetime of heartache. They won't know how to treat their wife or husband, how to hold down a job when things get hard, how to deal with a difficult boss, or how to handle life when things don't go their way.

It may not be easy to hear, but it's the truth: a lack of discipline invites a curse and is anything but loving.

Discipline is Spiritual

When it comes right down to it, discipline is a spiritual practice.

Satan and his minions thrive in rebellion. It's the whole reason they were thrown out of God's presence (see Revelation 12:9). They don't care about your children any more than they care about you, and they don't play fair. Just as they want to draw you away from God through rebellion, they want to draw your children away from God and into rebellion, too—rebellion against you, your wife, and God. If you allow your children to become rebellious and to make rebellion a way of life, it will invite destruction and draw them away from their heavenly Father. They'll rebel against God and His authority in their lives, and that will kill them spiritually.

....

> ...you have the spiritual authority to fight spiritual battles for them until they are ready to fight them for themselves. It's up to you, Dad, to take a stand against the darkness and bring life to your children.

....

As a dad, you have the spiritual authority to fight spiritual battles for them until they are ready to fight them for themselves. It's up to you, Dad, to take a stand against the darkness and bring life to your children.

Discipline Begins with Faith

Before we dive more into disciplining or discussing techniques, we need to first set the foundation for success: faith.

If you want to discipline your children correctly, you must discipline *by faith* with the help of the Holy Spirit. Disciplining *by faith* means starting your discipline with the Word. If parenting is like gardening, and disciplining is like tending that garden, then part of tending the garden is sowing the right kind of seed.

Jesus talked about the importance of sowing in His parable of the sower:

> *"A farmer went out to sow his seed. As he was scattering the seed, some fell along the path; it was trampled on, and the birds ate it up. Some fell on rocky ground, and when it came up, the plants withered because they had no moisture. Other seed fell among thorns, which grew up with it and choked the plants. Still other seed fell on good soil. It came up and yielded a crop, a hundred times more than was sown."...* (Luke 8:5-8).

You, Dad, are a farmer who is constantly sowing into your children's lives. You sow good seeds into them by training them in the things of God. It's your responsibility to sow the Word into them by reading the Bible with them and over them, by teaching them what it says and how it applies to their lives, and by praying for them.

....

You must sow the Word into the lives of your children. Every God-thing starts with faith, and that includes parenting. Have faith that the seeds you sow into your children will reap a good harvest.

....

This is a key step, not an afterthought. You *must* sow the Word into the lives of your children. Every God-thing starts with faith, and that includes parenting. Have faith that the seeds you sow into your children will reap a good harvest. Even if they walk away for a season, you can know—and confidently declare—that they'll come back because they have the seeds of God's Word that you've sown deep inside them.

Discipline Rises Out of Love

One of my wife's and my favorite verses is, "...love covers a multitude of sins" (1 Peter 4:8). That's good news and an important key to discipline. Your children must be convinced that you love them before you can successfully discipline them. They need to hear it, see it, and know it.

I talked about the 90-10 principle in chapter 8. There, I applied it to words, but it applies to all of parenting. Ninety-percent of parenting should be spent loving on your children with your words and actions. That means building them up, encouraging them, praying for them, and sacrificing for them. Only ten-percent of your words should be spent on discipline and correction.

If you'll put this 90-10 principle into practice, your children will accept discipline and correction when it comes. Pain is a necessary part of discipline, but if children receive pain or suffering from a person that they know loves them, they won't rebel against it. If you try to discipline without love, however, it will breed rebellion *every time.*

Now that we've laid the foundation for why discipline is important and what it is, let's look at the top goals of discipline.

Goal #1: Teach Responsibility

The first goal of discipline is to teach personal responsibility. If you don't teach your children to take personal responsibility for their lives, they'll always be victims. They'll always be controlled by someone else's choices. They'll always feel "it's not *my* fault." That's why it's so important to teach your children to take responsibility for their own actions and

THE WHAT AND WHY OF DISCIPLINE

destiny. Help them see that only the Lord should dictate their destinies—no one else. They're not victims but fully in control of what they say and do; and it's from those actions that they receive consequences, good or bad.

Goal #2: Drive Out Selfishness

Selfishness is prevalent in our culture. It's at the root of many divorces and one of the main reasons so many people don't want to become parents. In both cases, people decide that marriage and parenting are "too taxing." They don't want anyone or anything getting in the way of them focusing their lives on themselves. It's selfishness, pure and simple.

As a father, you have a responsibility to drive selfishness out of your children. You've got to teach them to share. You've got to teach them to give because giving is a spiritual principle. Raise them with the understanding that giving always leads to receiving more. When they give their lives to help others—including a spouse and children—they'll be blessed. Teach them that.

One of the best lessons I ever taught my children had to do with this very topic. They were complaining about their toys one day.

"I'm bored, Daddy. I don't have anything to do. I don't have anything to play with. It's your job to entertain us, Daddy." They acted like I was some kind of sideshow!

I didn't say a word. I just got a big box and started loading up their toys.

"Why are you taking all of our toys?"

"Well, I'm taking them to give them to someone who wants to play with them."

"NO, NO, NO!" It's amazing how quickly they became thankful for what they had.

We need to rid our children of selfishness. There are too many problems in our society caused by it, and we want better for our children.

From Caleb, my second oldest son:

> *There were many benefits to having Family Time each night.*
>
> *First and foremost, the reading of the Bible as a group allowed us, the children, to see our father place value in the Word. It let us know that the Word was a priority in my father's life and that we should make it a priority in ours as well.*
>
> *Second, it forced us to think each and every day about what we were truly grateful for. Dad would not let us just give superficial answers. If one of us didn't put any thought into our answer, he had us try again. In today's world, it is so easy to complain about our jobs or what the neighbors have that we don't. We soon discovered that saying out loud what we were thankful for created an environment for peace and joy no matter the circumstances.*

Goal #3: Respect for Authority

Nowadays, people seem to have a general lack of respect for authority; and, as a parent, another goal of discipline is to counter that disrespect.

One of my sons is an award-winning teacher in the school system. He told me that teachers are usually blamed for students' misdeeds. Parents often come in to parent-teacher conferences and say, "That can't be my child. You're mistreating little Johnny." It doesn't matter if little Johnny misbehaved or acted a fool. They want to know, "What did *you* do to make little Johnny act like that?!"

This is the kind of attitude that comes from parents who never learned respect for authority themselves. It's also an example of the attitude, *"Nobody's gonna tell me what to do."* It's dangerous and destructive!

There's protection under authority. Every one of us has someone we answer to: spiritual leaders, pastors, government officials, and bosses. When we submit to that spiritual and physical authority, we have protection. You need to train your kids in this truth. If you want them to fulfill their destinies, you must teach them to respect authority, too.

Return to the Vision

If you want your children to behave well, to have self-control and know how to handle themselves in public and in life, it requires effort at home when they're young. It requires discipline. Don't wait until they're throwing food in a restaurant or a fit in school to discipline them. Be proactive. Teach them responsibility, selflessness, and respect for authority. Return to your vision and let that be your motivation. Remember what your goal is—what you want for them in life. Then match your discipline to accomplish that goal.

Key Points

1. Unruly children were never God's intention, and discipline is what keeps them from getting there. Disciplining your children allows them to be the blessings they were intended to be.
2. Discipline is love. If you don't discipline your children, you don't love them.
3. Parenting is 90% building up your children with words and actions and 10% correction.
4. Disciplining a child without first demonstrating to that child that you love him or her will only lead to rebellion.
5. The goals of discipline are to build personal responsibility, drive out selfishness, and teach respect for authority to your children. All these goals lead to healthier, more fulfilling, and more rewarding lives.

Discussion Questions

1. Why is discipline an act of love?
2. What is the difference between discipline and abuse?
3. Have you ever felt guilty for disciplining your children? Why or why not?

4. Why is the 90-10 principle important for effective discipline?
5. Why must you teach personal responsibility to your children? What are some ways to do that?
6. How can you drive out selfishness from your children?
7. How is respect for authority something learned? How can you teach it to your children?

Take Action

Read the following verses. Meditate on and pray for God to help you better understand them and apply them to your children. Then write down the direction the Holy Spirit gives you. Return to these verses and the Holy Spirit's instructions regularly.

- *Don't fail to discipline your children. The rod of punishment won't kill them. Physical discipline may well save them from death* (Proverbs 23:13-14 NLT).
- *The rod and rebuke give wisdom, but a child left to himself brings shame to his mother* (Proverbs 29:15 NKJV).
- *Train up a child in the way he should go, and when he is old he will not depart from it* (Proverbs 22:6 NKJV).

10

How to Discipline

No discipline seems pleasant at the time, but painful. Later on, however, it produces a harvest of righteousness and peace for those who have been trained by it.
(Hebrews 12:11)

In the last chapter, I talked about why discipline is important and why we must begin our discipline with faith. We also learned the three goals of discipline: to build responsibility, drive out selfishness, and teach respect for authority. In this chapter, we're going to talk about *how* to discipline.

There is no one identical way to discipline every child. Each person is different, so discipline differs for every child. With eleven boys, believe me when I say I've run the full gamut of personalities and ages that need disciplining. Some children are sensitive and easily corrected, others tough and headstrong. Thankfully, there are many resources to choose from.

Your Discipline Tool Box

Dad, you have a tool box full of techniques that you can use to discipline and train your children. This is by no means a comprehensive list, but some of the ones I've used are:

- **Spanking**

    It's controversial, but the Word of God clearly endorses it. Spanking is beneficial when there is a clear incident of rebellion. If I give my son a command or he's been told to do or not to do something repeatedly and then decides to disobey, it's clear rebellion. That's an example of when spanking is warranted.

- **Words**

    A stern talking to or a discussion about cause and effect works with some children, especially older children who can grasp the principles you're trying to convey.

- **Restitution**

    When something has been broken, destroyed, or lost, have them clean up and replace what they broke. I did this when one of my boys decided it was a good idea to smash our neighbors' mailboxes.

- **Writing Scripture**

    When they're old enough, make them copy the book of Proverbs by hand. Not only is it a difficult task, but it'll get the Word in them at the same time. I used this technique when my children disrespected their teachers.

- **Taking Something Away**
  When you withhold something your child values (i.e. toys, bikes, car, attendance to a special event, etc.), it teaches them to appreciate the toys and privileges they have.
- **Services or Work**
  Give your kids special assignments where they donate their time and service to their family or others.
- **Sitting Still**
  Determine a place and a period of time and make them sit still. This can be a tougher punishment than spanking for younger children.

These are just a few discipline techniques that I've used. Regardless of which technique you use, be careful. Don't fall into the common trap of threatening your children with discipline but then never following through.

So often parents will say, "If you do that *one more time*, I'm going to…"

Your children will quickly learn that your threats are empty, and your words will become meaningless. Threats of discipline are *not* discipline.

Remember, the discipline needs to hurt in some way in order to get their attention. This is vital. You must get their attention, or you've wasted your time. I also fit the discipline to the child—to his personality and age—and I take into consideration how unaware he was and/or how flat-out dumb or childish the action was.

As I've already said, spanking is necessary when rebellion is present. If a child ignores what he knows to do or not do, and it's a clear instance of rebellion, then he or she receives a spanking.

Other times, I would take something away. For example, my teenager once told my wife and me that he was going out in his car to a specific location. We later found out he went several other places, too, and never let us know. It was an omission that broke our family's rules. The consequence was that he lost access to his car and his phone for two weeks. Because of his age and his personality, that discipline was significant. It hurt.

Another son, at a much younger age, had a hard time sitting still during our Family Time of reading the Word. Therefore, he had to sit on my lap, and I held him still until he stopped wriggling. It was painful for a little boy who seemed to have ants in his pants, but he soon learned self-control.

....
Successful discipline requires that you win every time.
....

Other children respond to a stern talk. They're sensitive and quick to repent and correct their behaviors.

In all these instances, I tailored the discipline to the individual child, and in every instance, I won. I'm not being glib or cocky. Successful discipline requires that you win every time. If you don't persist until you win, you do two things. First, you make it harder on yourself next time. Your children will begin testing you at every turn. And second, it gives them over to rebellion which, as I've already mentioned, is a dangerous place for your children to be. It sets them on a self-destructive path.

Then, no matter what the method of discipline, there are several keys that apply across the board. Let's look at those now.

Start Early

Disciplining at a young age is easy because small children innately respect your authority. If you wait until your children are 6, 8, or 10 years old, you are in for a big fight. Have you ever seen a toddler reach for something he's been told several times not to grab? As he reaches for it, he slowly turns around and looks at you. He's testing the waters, trying to see what you are going to do.

Don't let toddlers fool you, they know they're doing something wrong. That's the moment to start disciplining them. Communication is one of the last developmental milestones. They may not be able to speak yet, but—you'd better believe it—they understand what they're doing. So, don't wait. Get started early!

Of course, if your children are older, I'm not suggesting that it's too late. It's never too late. Yes, it will be harder than if they were toddlers, but start where you are. You can't change the past, but you can change the future. The important thing is to simply start.

Be Consistent

Consistency is a huge key to success in parenting. If they're little, don't count to three before you expect them to obey. Teach them that you're true to your word, and you will follow through on the discipline you've established—*every* time. Be clear about your expectations and what will happen if they disobey. Let them know that the choice is theirs.

> ...discipline is as much a spiritual battle for
> the souls of your children as it is about
> teaching them proper behavior.

You want them to trust what you say, in that moment and in the future. If you don't follow through, then you're teaching them that rebellion is acceptable. Remember, discipline is as much a spiritual battle for the souls of your children as it is about teaching them proper behavior. Rebellion is a satanic spirit that will cost them greatly. Don't allow it at any level.

For example, if my child does something he shouldn't do, I might say, "I want you to understand that you're making a bad choice, and it's unacceptable. I love you too much to let you act like that; so if you do that again, I'm going to (<u>fill in the blank</u>)." The wrongdoing will determine the discipline.

Then, I have them repeat it back to me. I'll ask, "What did I just tell you?"

"You told me if I do that, you're going to…"

"That's right. I don't want to punish you. I don't like it at all. So, if I do have to punish you, whose fault is it?"

Taking them through this question and answer process teaches them personal responsibility. I make it clear that I would rather play and have a good time, but if they choose to disobey, there will be consequences. It's their choice.

In our home, I start teaching them what is and isn't acceptable at a young age. It doesn't take them long to learn that disrespecting their mother—my wife—is a nonstarter. They also know that complaining about what they do or don't have is not allowed. I've been overseas and have seen how blessed my children are. My children—and quite probably yours—have nothing to complain about. They also learn at a young age to sit still while our family reads the Word. If they want to wriggle, they get to sit on my lap while I hold them still. These may seem like small issues, but my children have all learned early what I will and won't allow. They've also learned quickly that I follow through on what I say. This makes for fewer battles when they're older.

Be in Unity

In addition to consistency in discipline, you want to be sure you have unity between mom and dad.

"Well, Daddy said..." or "But Momma said..." won't cut it.

Surely, you've heard that. Your beautiful children can be conniving little things, can't they? That's very common. Kids will almost always try—at least once—to get their way by driving a wedge between you and your wife. That's why, as a parental unit, you have to commit to being in unity.

Psalm 133 states, "How good and pleasant it is when God's people live together in unity! ...For there the LORD bestows his blessing, even life forevermore."

Together as parents, you both need to come into unity about the roles you each take, and the standards your family holds. As the father, you need to be the lead disciplinarian, and your wife needs to respect that position. Then both of you need to protect each other by not letting your children speak badly about the other parent or bring division. This creates unity.

Invite the Holy Spirit to Help You

In the last chapter, I talked about how discipline begins with faith, and I want to dive into that a bit more. Every Spirit-filled father needs to accept that the Holy Spirit can do a much better job than he can. And He will, if we'll invite Him.

There have been many times when I've been sitting in my chair or laying in my bed, and all of a sudden, the Holy Spirit will speak to me about one of my boys.

On one particular occasion, He woke me up and said, "Go to the house your son said he was going to spend the night."

When I arrived, my son wasn't there. Remember, my children aren't perfect. They're kids. Once in a while they try to pull one over on Dear Ole Dad. Thankfully, the Holy Spirit loves my son enough to not let him get away with lying to me—and I love the Holy Spirit enough to listen.

Dad, if you'll invite Him, the Holy Spirit will help you. When you pray over your children, you're inviting the Holy Spirit to help them *and* you. You're calling forth their destinies. I encourage you to pray for them out loud, where your children can hear you. Don't just do it in secret. Pray over them while they are in the room with you, and even while they are in bed or asleep. Praying and inviting the Holy Spirit to be involved is the most important part of discipline. Please don't skip this step.

Yes, I discipline my children. Yes, I talk with them and make my expectations clear. Yes, I choose the kind of discipline that best fits the offense and the child. But most importantly, I pray and invite the Holy Spirit to lead me as I do it.

Does that mean I'm perfect or that I've never made mistakes? Of course not. But with the help of the Holy Spirit, I've made fewer mistakes than I would have without Him.

....
...*always* follow discipline with expressions of love.
....

Follow Discipline with Expressions of Love
Finally, in addition to consistency, unity, and asking for the Holy Spirit's help when you discipline, there's one more element to proper discipline—and it happens *after* you discipline. You should *always* follow discipline with expressions of love. This is a time to settle things once and for all so you can both move forward. Here are the steps I take after I have disciplined one of my sons:

1. Hug him. If my son has received a spanking and is crying, I hold him while he cries.
2. Make him apologize for his wrongdoing. This allows him to take personal responsibility for what he did.
3. Forgive him. Let him know that he is forgiven.
4. Shower him with words of affirmation. For instance, I tell my son, "You're a good boy. I love you and will

never leave you. I'm not disappointed in you. I didn't like that choice, but I'm never disappointed in you."
5. Leave the incident in the past. Once the discipline is over, it's over. I never bring it up again.

I look at discipline as an interruption of the love train that my boys and I are on. Like the Word tells us, "...weeping may stay for the night, but rejoicing comes in the morning" (Psalm 30:5). We never want to stay in the place of discipline for long. We, instead, want to get back on the love train and keep moving.

As I close this chapter, I want to reiterate the need for the Holy Spirit's leading in your parenting and in your disciplining. By allowing Him to work in and through you, you're more likely to give your children what they need. No, you won't be perfect, but you'll approach your role from a godly worldview and be more prepared to reflect the Father's heart.

Key Points

1. Every dad has a tool box of discipline techniques at his disposal. Find what works for each of your children.
2. Begin disciplining as soon as your children understand right from wrong, which is usually when they're toddlers.
3. Be consistent. Never threaten. Set discipline and follow through.
4. Be in unity with your wife. Understand, respect, and protect each of your roles.
5. Invite the Holy Spirit to help you parent. He knows best.
6. Always follow discipline with expressions of love.
7. Once the discipline is over, it's over. Never bring up your child's wrongdoing again.

Discussion Questions

1. When was the first time you remember disciplining your child? What instigated it? What was the result of it? Was it effective?
2. What role do you and your wife play in disciplining your children? How do you respect one another's roles? How can you better support one another?

3. Why is it important to follow discipline with acts of love?
4. What do you teach your children about their heavenly Father when you discipline them?

Take Action

Consider each of your children. What discipline techniques have you used? Have they worked? How can you discipline more effectively in the future? Name three changes you'd like to make to the way you discipline your children.

1. _____
   _____
   _____

2. _____
   _____
   _____

3. _____
   _____
   _____

11

Destructive Worldviews in Discipline

*Do not conform to the pattern of this world,
but be transformed by the renewing of your mind.
Then you will be able to test and approve what God's
will is—his good, pleasing and perfect will.*
(Romans 12:2)

Often, adults enter parenting with the wrong kind of thinking. Without realizing it, they allow destructive worldviews to change the way they parent and relate to their children. Taking on one of these worldviews is dangerous and serves no one—not you, and definitely not your children. These worldviews often leave children without the spiritual and emotional covering they need.

I've battled with all the incorrect ways of thinking we're going to look at in this chapter, and I am reminded, once again, that fatherhood is not for wimps. As a dad, you must be willing to let God reveal your faults and help you change for your own peace of mind and for the future of your children.

Here are four destructive worldviews that are common among modern-day parents.

"I want to be their friend."

Sorry, Dad, God called you to be a parent, not a friend. Many parents have holes in their own hearts from past hurts that they try to use their children to heal. The result? They don't want to discipline. They don't want to make unpopular decisions, or they are unwilling to follow through with discipline. They try to be their children's friend instead of their parent.

Don't let that be you.

The day will come when your children are grown and you'll be able to be friends, but you're called to be their father *first*, knowing what is best for them even when they don't. During the formative years, you'll require them to do things, say things, and eat things that they may not want to do, say, or eat. Many of my boys are older and married now, and we have great friendships; but for those who are still at home and under my care, I am Dad first.

One example of an unpopular decision for our family is spending the night with friends. Because of incidents that happened at friends' houses when my wife and I were children, we have a no-spend-the-night policy in our home until our boys are teenagers. Even then, we talk about it. It's not a popular choice, but I don't care. I can't protect them at somebody else's house. I don't mind going to get them late, but we don't let them spend the night. I want to protect my kids until they grow older and are mature enough to handle

DESTRUCTIVE WORLDVIEWS IN DISCIPLINE

challenging situations themselves. We've enforced this rule for the last 20 years. It's not always popular, but it's a rule for our family. You may have different rules for your family. The point is, each of us dads are responsible for our children. *We are in charge, not them.*

From Jonathan ("Jon Jon"), my fourth oldest son:

My girlfriend and I had been dating for a year and a half, and I was praying about asking her to marry me. Through a friend of a friend, I learned she had cheated on me. I confronted her. She confessed to cheating, said she was very sorry, and seemed genuinely remorseful about what she had done.

Devastated, I was unsure how to handle the situation. I wrestled with the idea of giving her a second chance, desperate to believe that she was sincere and would never cheat again. I wanted to trust her so badly.

I went to my dad. He looked me straight in the eyes and said, "If you trust her and get back with her, you are an idiot and going completely against my will."

He didn't say that because he hated or even disliked her, but she had proven herself untrustworthy. He wanted to protect me from getting hurt again. He wanted me to take some time to allow her to earn and deserve my trust, not jump back into a potentially hurtful situation. I was angry and hurt by his response, but I listened. I broke up with her, fully anticipating that our time apart would be short.

But Dad was right. My ex-girlfriend and I parted ways.

I still remember that conversation and how honest and straightforward Dad was. He wasn't angry. He didn't demand that I do what he wanted me to do. Breaking up with her was still my choice. If he had beaten around the bush and been less straightforward, I may not have listened. But that wasn't Dad's style. He was logical. He was impossible to argue with. And, deep down, I knew he was right.

Looking back, I appreciate his honesty and how he was willing to tell me what I needed to hear, instead of what I wanted to hear. It taught me that parents have to put aside the desire to be their child's friend and, instead, step up and be a parent. To guide and protect their children, parents must be willing to be honest and tell them hard truths.

Today, I'm married to an amazing woman, and we have our own son. I know when the time comes, I'll be ready to speak truth to him even if it's difficult for him to hear, just as my dad did to me. I'll be ready because I'll be his dad first.

"They're just kids. One day they'll grow out of it."

One statement serves as the basis for all my discipline: *"I love you too much to let you act like that."* It's a statement I say to

DESTRUCTIVE WORLDVIEWS IN DISCIPLINE

my children often. I let them know that I love them too much to turn the other way and allow childishness, selfishness, or rebellion to continue. To do so is laziness, and laziness and parenting don't go together. Our children are too important to be left alone. They want their dad to show up and be their dad. When you do that—when you train and discipline them out of love—your children will receive it. They may not like it, but they will receive it.

....

You want your children to be dreamers, to go after whatever God has for them. But you also want them to submit to authority, because without it, they'll invite a world of unnecessary pain into their lives and have a hard time finding success.

....

"I don't want to break their will."
It's fine to break their wills—especially when their will is to be rebellious and have it their way all the time. What you don't want to break are their spirits. Discipline teaches children to submit to legitimate authority, not to make them into robots.

You want your children to be dreamers, to go after whatever God has for them. But you also want them to submit to authority, because without it, they'll invite a world of unnecessary pain into their lives and have a hard time finding success. Discipline gives them the tools they need (i.e. self-control, self-discipline, respect for authority, etc.) to succeed in life and in all God has for them. Disciplining your children helps them discover the fine line between having respect for others, but also being true to who God has created them to be.

"Do as I say, not as I do."

The "do as I say, not as I do" mantra doesn't cut it as a parenting technique. Your children are watching you. They're watching to see if you're consistent and a person of your word. They're watching to see how you treat your wife. One day they'll treat their wives—or expect to be treated as a wife—the same way.

Behavior teaches more than words. Discipline breaks down when we, as dads, don't model what we try to teach our kids. If we want them to pay attention to our words, we have to model and practice what we preach.

Dad, all these mentalities and thought processes run rampant in our culture. Many dads mistakenly think being their children's friend, or refusing to address issues, will lead to well-adjusted, mature adults. Or, they assume that breaking their children's wills is a bad thing. Or worse, they

DESTRUCTIVE WORLDVIEWS IN DISCIPLINE

demand more from their children than they do from themselves. How can anyone expect these approaches to work? Using them only abandons children and leaves them without the support and guidance they need.

Instead, stand up and be the dad your children need you to be. The Holy Spirit can and will help you. He can help you identify and correct these destructive worldviews.

Key Points

1. You are called to be your children's dad *first*, then later their friend—when they're grown.
2. Break their will, not their spirit. When you discipline your children, you are preparing them for what God calls them to be. Discipline done in love will never lead to fear and insecurity.
3. Model the kind of behavior you expect from your children. Your actions will always speak louder than your words.
4. Let them know that you love them too much to allow them to behave badly.

Discussion Questions

1. Have you ever tried to be your child's friend instead of their parent? What was the result?
2. Why is it necessary to address destructive behaviors instead of thinking your children will eventually grow out of them?
3. What is the difference between a child's will and spirit? Why is it OK to break their will but not their spirit?
4. Are there areas in which you have applied the "do as I say, not as I do" approach? What did your children learn from this?

Take Action

Ask the Holy Spirit to bring to your mind any ungodly behaviors or attitudes that you have allowed your children to have that need to be addressed. Write them down and plan ways to begin addressing them. Then ask the Holy Spirit to bring to your mind any behaviors or attitudes that you need to change, especially those where you have taken a "do as I say, not as I do" position.

SECTION 3
DEVELOPING
REAL CHARACTER

It was the South State Championship, one of the biggest high school games in Mississippi's history. Our school was set to play against Wayne County, and my oldest son, Micah, a senior at the time, was the quarterback. He had led his team through an undefeated season. Our whole community rallied behind the team.

There was just one problem: Micah had blown out his knee, severely damaging his ACL, MCL, and meniscus in the last game of the regular season. The doctor told us he couldn't hurt it any more than it was already hurt but playing on it would be painful. *Really* painful.

I'll never forget the moment Micah looked into my eyes and said, "Dad, I want to finish."

WOW!

I bought him one of those big knee braces and prayed.

The opponents, Wayne County, had a big, tough team that liked to hit hard. Time and again during the playoff games I winced as I watched Micah get hit...but he always got back up. Then in the fourth quarter, there was a big pile up and Micah was at the bottom. He tried to get up but couldn't. Physically, he had given all he had to give.

From the bleachers, I couldn't do anything but watch him struggle. I knew he was in pain. I also knew he couldn't hurt his knee any worse than it already was. He had come this far, and for his sake, I didn't want him to stop short. He *needed* to finish.

"GET UP!" I shouted. "You have to finish what you started!"

Micah struggled to his feet. It wasn't his physical strength that was going to get him through the end of the game. It was a sheer test of character…a test Micah passed.

Talent, ability, and personality will get you in the door, but character keeps you there. A major problem today is that people have a lot of talent but no character. This deficiency affects every part of society: marriage, business, politics—it all crumbles under the weight of a society without character.

Character is one of those things that's hard to define. It can be described by words like *honest* and *trustworthy*, but it's more than that. It's the ability to stand for what is right—sometimes all by yourself and oftentimes when no one is looking. It's being able to look at yourself and be brutally honest with what you see.

Character is that "something" inside you that makes you uncomfortable with a lie. It makes you do a good job no matter how much you get paid.

Character makes you keep going when the odds are against you. It makes you finish what you start.

Our country has lost its sense of character because fathers aren't around anymore to give it to their children and model it in front of them, but I believe we can change that. I believe *you* can change that.

In this section, we'll look at some key ingredients of character.

12

Take Responsibility

"Who told you that you were naked?" the LORD God asked. "Have you eaten from the tree whose fruit I commanded you not to eat?" The man replied, "It was the woman you gave me who gave me the fruit, and I ate it." Then the LORD God asked the woman, "What have you done?" "The serpent deceived me," she replied. "That's why I ate it."
(Genesis 3:11-13 NLT)

From the very beginning of time, mankind has been making excuses for his actions and shirking his responsibility. And it's still going on today. People who resist taking responsibility always have an excuse. They're quick to blame others for their mistakes or play the victim card when their lives are in shambles. It's a habit that starts young.

When one of my sons was six years old, he played baseball for the first time. He played in the seven-and-eight-year-old league, mainly because I hate T-ball.

Now when it comes to sports, I'm not one of those crazy parents who expects perfection. They're *kids*. They will make mistakes; but they have to be aware of their mistakes so they can work on them during practice.

In one game, the batter hit a ball to my son...and he missed it. My wife screamed out, "That's OK, baby. You tried!"

Being one of the coaches, I stood up and yelled, "Come on, man! You have to catch that!"

In moments like these, there's a definite difference between the way Mom and Dad react! Of course, kids need both.

My son looked at me, took off his brand-new glove, and threw it to the ground. He grumbled, "Stupid glove!" It wasn't the glove's fault, but to my six-year-old's mind, it was easier to blame the glove than himself. It was an excuse.

Sadly, I see that same attitude in many adults because they didn't have a father to tell them, "Don't make excuses." People are blaming others for their poor decisions or lack of success instead of standing up and taking responsibility.

....

Jesus is willing to accept a repentant spirit. Nothing that hell has invented is more powerful than the blood of Jesus; but if you make excuses, you will never allow yourself to get clean.

....

This is an issue that floods our society. Today's society tells people that they're victims; and, as a result, we accept their bad behavior, excuse their lack of effort, and allow someone else to be blamed for their choices. I have a deep respect for people in today's world who stand up and admit when they're wrong.

This is also true from a spiritual perspective. To know the forgiveness that the blood of Jesus paid for on the cross, we must ask for forgiveness and repent. If we're making excuses for bad behavior and choices, we'll never do that. Like David said in Psalm 51, we must be willing to say, "It's me, Lord. I am wrong."

People in our churches are full of guilt and shame because they never get clean. Jesus is willing to accept a repentant spirit. Nothing that hell has invented is more powerful than the blood of Jesus; but if you make excuses, you will never allow yourself to get clean.

It may seem like a small thing, but letting my little boy blame his glove sows a seed of not accepting responsibility in his life, and I won't have that.

Taking Responsibility Affects Destiny

Another equally important aspect of personal responsibility is how it affects a child's destiny. As I mentioned in chapter 3, God has a great plan not only for us, but also for our children. He will give us opportunities to walk in our destiny, but every one of us has to take responsibility to grab those opportunities and do something with them. How far we go is God's business, but *going* is *our* business.

After blaming the glove for his troubles, my six-year-old said, "Dad, I want to be good."

That's what I like to hear. I offered to practice with him on a regular basis. By doing so, I did my part by giving him the opportunity to improve so that he could achieve the level of ballplaying he desired. That said, following through with the practice was on him. He had to lay down the video games, turn off the television, and come outside to throw the ball with me. That was his responsibility.

So many people want to have great abilities, but are unwilling to put in the work to develop them. They are offered opportunities to learn, work, and improve, but those things aren't automatic. They must have character and take personal responsibility to make their dreams happen.

Understanding this starts young.

Dad, it's your job to teach your children that they can achieve great things—but no one is going to wrap their dream up with a bow and give it to them. They must work for it. You must teach them to:

- *Believe in God.*
- *Believe in themselves.*
- *Take advantage of opportunities when they arise.*
- *Realize that achieving great things is their choice. It's their life. And it's their destiny.*

TAKE RESPONSIBILITY

From Micah, my oldest son:

The kids' bathroom had become a work of art...or at least a labor of love. Our amazing mom had lovingly and painstakingly planned and decorated it, transforming it into a colorful and fun place for us.

Then the unthinkable happened.

One of the younger boys left the top off the toothpaste... and the baby had found it. It was the exact "paint" he needed to do a little redecorating of his own. Mom's masterpiece became a smeared mess of bubble gum toothpaste.

That's when Dad got involved. He demanded to know who had left the top off the toothpaste. When no one admitted his mistake, in effect lying by omission, Dad began disciplining us one by one. He started with me, the oldest, and worked his way down the line. Then Dad reached brother number 6.

"It was me," number 6 confessed, just before receiving his spanking. He was the one who had left the top of the toothpaste and had even stood by as the rest of us took his punishment. We still give him a hard time about that!

My dad stopped, looked at him, realization dawning that he had punished those of us who were innocent. "Go help your mother clean it up," he said.

Those of us who had already been spanked stood there with tear-streaked faces and mouths wide open. We laugh about it now and love to pick on Dad about his mistake, but I learned a valuable lesson that day. It wasn't the discipline that I remember, it was what came next.

Later that night, during Family Time, my dad looked each boy in the eye, called us by name, and said, "I'm sorry. Daddy was wrong. Can you forgive me?"

Wow!

My dad is 6'2, 275lbs. He dwarfed us, and yet he was asking for our forgiveness. He had made a mistake, and he admitted it. And more than that, he asked for our forgiveness. I have never forgotten that lesson: as a man, no matter what, if you have wronged someone, make it right.

> Your children will learn more from your example than from a lecture.

Follow Jesus's Example

Personal responsibility is something Jesus modeled in His life. He never let anything, or anybody, distract Him from His destiny. Even close friends like Peter, who tried to distract Jesus from His destiny on the cross, couldn't stop Him. Where do you think Jesus got His focus and determination? It came from His Father loving on Him. It came from His

TAKE RESPONSIBILITY

Father praising Him. It came from His Father giving Him identity and purpose.

You can also teach your children by your example. One way I do this is by taking responsibility for my mistakes and apologizing to my children when I'm wrong. I'm not going to lie—it's difficult to apologize to a 7-year-old because you told him you'd do something that you ended up not being able to do. But it's worth the discomfort when you realize you're teaching them how to own up to their mistakes. Your children will learn more from your example than from a lecture.

Dad, take responsibility for your children and make sure they learn early on to take responsibility for their lives.

Key Points

1. Teach your children not to be victims! Help them understand that every person is responsible for his or her own God-given life.
2. Excuses reveal a lack of character. Allowing people (even your children) to make excuses keeps them from achieving all that God created them to achieve.
3. For children, admitting when they're wrong is a necessary step in accepting responsibility and in accepting salvation.
4. Your children will learn to take responsibility from watching your example. So, don't make excuses for your mistakes, and, if warranted, ask them for forgiveness.

Discussion Questions

1. Why is accepting personal responsibility so important?
2. Have you encountered someone who refused to take responsibility for their actions? How did this affect them, their work, or their future?
3. Why is personal responsibility so important to salvation?

All the family including our first grandson Seth

7 boys, 10 years old and under

Mom loved dressing them alike

Florida vacation, 2008

Family photo shoot, Hickman style

Our attempt at a bad sweater Christmas

Family photo shoot, 2010

We could take over a
golf course!

Love Ole Miss football games

Family ski trip, 2013

Whole family at Ben's high school graduation, 2013

Caleb and Jacob graduation from Ole Miss, 2014

Skiing in Colorado, 2013

Micah, the first boy to get married, 2014

Mandeville High School football game with Micah, Caleb, and Dad

Samuel's high school graduation, 2014

Big Al

Amy and Matthew

Sunday morning after church

Josiah and Elisha at baseball, 2016

The whole family in Destin, 2017 – we are growing!

Samuel and Matthew on rare snow day in Mississippi

Josiah, Elisha, Isaac, and Nathan always looking to golf

Nathan and Matthew – we love to fish

Older brothers presenting Nathan at his Rite of Passage ceremony

Rite of Passage ceremony, 2018

Josiah's graduation from PRCC, 2018

Samuel with one of our granddaughters, 2017

Micah with our 1st grandson, 2015

(Left) Josiah and Samuel at Josiah's wedding, 2018

(Below, from left to right) Nathan, Jonathan, Matthew, Elisha, Isaac, Josiah, Micah, Caleb, Samuel, Jacob, and Benjamin. All my boys.

Matthew and Dad watching big brother practice

Allen and Amy 2019, still sane after 11 boys and all these years!

4. How can you teach personal responsibility to your children? Give a specific example, like the baseball story I shared above.

Take Action

Think of a time when your children tried to shirk their responsibility. How did you respond? Did you correct them, or did you accept their excuses? Consider how you would handle the situation differently now.

13

Never Quit. Persevere.

But the fruit of the Spirit is love, joy, peace, forbearance, kindness, goodness, faithfulness, gentleness and self-control. Against such things there is no law.
(Galatians 5:22-23)

Perseverance has almost become an outdated notion in today's society. If anything is hard, or if it doesn't come easy on the first try, we quit.

Galatians 5:22-23 tells us perseverance is a fruit of the Spirit. *Perseverance* in the Greek can be translated as "long-suffering, endurance, and patience." Every one of us—you, me, and our children—need a healthy dose of perseverance in our lives.

....

When I would discipline my children, I'd often say to myself, "I'm going to win." Why?...My kids needed me to win.

....

Perseverance starts with dads. When I would discipline my children, I'd often say to myself, "I'm going to win." Why?

Because, I knew that I was fighting for them to have a great future. I couldn't afford to lose the battle. Even when the outcome didn't look good, I would keep going. I would push through. I would keep fighting.

My kids *needed* me to win.

Perseverance Versus Hard-headedness

Some people might mistake perseverance for hard-headedness, but there's a big difference between the two. Perseverance is about staying the course because you have something worth fighting for. Hard-headedness is being stubborn for no reason other than you just don't want to do something. That's quite a difference!

Let me give you an example. My oldest son was very strong-willed, which is a positive thing if developed and matured appropriately. As his father, it was my job to help develop and set the course for him to mature positively as a strong-willed boy.

I still remember that moment when he was young, when he made eye contact with his mother then tipped his glass over *on purpose*. She cleaned up the mess and told him not to do it again. Then I stepped in.

For 22 nights in a row, he did the same thing! I disciplined him each time. Each night I told him, "I love you too much to let you be rebellious." Then, I would say *to him*, "I'm going to win."

On the 23rd night, he held the glass in his hand, looked over at me, and set the glass back down instead of spilling it. I had done it. I had won. I had persevered.

Persevering in Life

Often kids receive what they want too easily. They don't know how to work for what they receive or endure adversity along the way to achieving their goals. A lack of perseverance plays out with horrible results that affect children's lives far into their adult years.

Take marriage for example. Good marriages don't just happen, you have to fight for them. Couples have to work through problems and issues. Or, what about providing for a family? All too often men put their families in a difficult situation by leaving their jobs when they encounter difficulties. This action, as an adult, is often the result of not being trained to persevere as a child.

When our kids' science projects are due, instead of finishing their projects ourselves, we need to make our children finish what they start. When we allow them to give up, we're setting a precedent that will follow them throughout their lives.

Does that mean you should never give your children anything without their earning it or that you shouldn't help them when they need it? Of course, not!

There are times, however, when they need to follow through with what they started—all the way to the end. It's in those moments that they're learning perseverance. Without that character trait—that fruit of the Spirit—they will *learn* to be quitters. They'll quit that sports team...that major in college...that marriage...and one day, they might just quit on their children. We want our children to be led by the Lord, not driven out of a good place because things got a little hard!

Dad, perseverance is a character trait that requires you to pay attention to your children's behavior. There's not a set of rules to make sure it develops in their lives. You must pick and choose the times you step in and help, and the times you don't. You must pray and follow God's leading, so you know the difference.

Key Points

1. Perseverance is a fruit of the Spirit.
2. As a father, you must *teach* your children to persevere. Adversity and trouble come to everyone. No one gets a free pass. So, teach your children to endure. It's not an automatic trait.
3. The most worthwhile things in life require perseverance. Whether it's raising world changers, succeeding in a career, or having a loving marriage, a person must fight through adversity.

Discussion Questions

1. Define perseverance in your own words.
2. In what ways have you seen a lack of perseverance shown in today's society?
3. Why is perseverance such an important character trait? And why should you put in the effort to persevere when it comes to building character in your children?
4. Why do you think God listed perseverance as a fruit of the Spirit among other traits like love, joy, and peace?

Take Action

Think of a time when your children have lacked perseverance. If it comes up again, what can you do to help them develop this fruit of the Holy Spirit in their lives?

14

Integrity Starts Young

The righteous who walks in his integrity—
blessed are his children after him!
(Proverbs 20:7 ESV)

One day, I was sitting downstairs in my chair when I heard a horrible sound.

"The house is on fire!" yelled one of my boys.

I jumped up and took the stairs double-time to find one of my sons trying to put out a fire on his mattress. There wasn't a second to lose. I launched into action.

A couple lessons I learned through that experience:

1. A queen-size mattress does not fit out of a standard-size window.
2. A mattress/box spring fire doesn't ever seem to die completely. Just when you think the flames are finally extinguished, they magically reignite.

Thinking that I had successfully put out the fire, I took the mattress and box spring downstairs and threw them out the back door. The moment they hit the grass, the mattress burst into flames again.

Just another day at the Hickman house.

IRREPLACEABLE

After the drama settled, I approached my eight-year-old son and asked the obvious question: "How in the world did your bed catch on fire?!"

His answer was fascinating. He said that sparks flew out from the electrical outlet nearby and caught the bed on fire. Uh-huh. Don't you love the workings of a child's mind? I'm sure to him that story sounded completely plausible.

Dad knew better.

It was time for a teachable moment. I investigated the socket where he said the sparks had come from and, of course, there were no black marks on or near it. I told my son I was going to call an electrician to come check it out for me, which would cost money. I explained that the electrician would be able to tell me if the socket was the source of the fire. I then asked my son if he was sure that his story was *exactly* what had happened.

"Yep," he said.

I left his room and headed back downstairs. As I walked, I asked quite loudly if someone could bring me the phone book. My plot to give him time to come clean worked.

He soon came downstairs with tears in his eyes and told me the truth. He had found a lighter and had used its flame to look for something under his bed. Ah yes, the workings of a child's mind.

Integrity is a Spiritual Principle

My eight-year-old had tried to get out of trouble by lying. He's not alone; that same inclination to avoid responsibility at any cost is prevalent in almost every facet of our world. Turn on the news and you'll witness the leaders of our country making stuff up as though the end justifies the means. Listen to the news media and it's clear, journalists no longer report the news. They invent it.

It's not easy to live with integrity in this culture, but it is a vital trait for our children's lives. Dad, we must teach our children to have integrity.

....

> Dad, we must be men of our word and train our children to be people of their word as well. If we want them to be the world changers God has called them to be, to impact the world for His glory, then teaching them to have integrity is foundational.

....

Why is having integrity important, especially when much of our society doesn't have a shred of it? Because having integrity is a spiritual principle.

The Bible calls Satan "the father of lies" (John 8:44). When we lie, we open a door for Satan to come and mess with us. Lies always make situations worse.

Dad, we must be men of our word and train our children to be people of their word as well. If we want them to be the world changers God has called them to be, to impact the world for His glory, then teaching them to have integrity is foundational.

I've said it before but it's worth repeating: you don't have to teach children to lie. They come into this world ready-made with that ability. Your job is to drive that lying inclination out of them, to demand integrity, to demand honesty, and to train them to be trustworthy.

Training Your Child in Integrity

Before you try to train your children to have integrity, you must live a life of integrity yourself. You can't say or model one thing and expect them to learn something else. If you make a promise, keep it. Sure, sometimes things happen that change what you committed or promised to do, but those occurrences should be few. That's why it's important to be intentional and careful about what you promise. Show your children what a man of integrity looks like.

All my boys have watched me pay the bills. I don't disclose the amounts to them, but I do let them see me make the payments so they can watch me handle my responsibilities. I want to demonstrate integrity in motion and disciple them through my example.

Another way I disciple them is to be aware of their childishness. When they were young, I didn't blindly trust them. I knew they weren't ready to be trusted. They were still learning to be men of their words. It grieves my heart to hear parents say their children never lie. To believe that is delusional. *They're children!*

That's another reason it's crucial that fathers take the lead in training their children to have integrity. In my experience, often mothers can't help but want to believe the absolute best of them. Moms can even have a difficult time questioning and calling them out on a lie, whereas dads have a natural ability to see past the emotion and deal with the issues at hand.

The Danger of Situational Ethics

When you realize that integrity is primarily a spiritual issue, you won't be quick to laugh at a little white lie. You'll realize your children's lives are at stake. To ignore those apparently minor indiscretions is to invite Satan's curse into their life.

Integrity extends into your children's work ethic, too. They must learn to be men and women of their word in their work. That means to work diligently and complete the jobs they've agreed to do to the best of their ability.

It bothers me when I hear people say, "I'm not getting paid enough for this."

If someone understood the job he was hired to do and agreed to do that job for a certain price, then he has no room to complain. He should do the job with integrity. Now, if an employer or client lied about what the job entailed, then he has a right to speak up; but, if he understood the job, agreed to do it, and agreed to the pay, then he should finish the job without complaint. That's integrity, and God rewards it.

From Jonathan ("Jon Jon"), my fourth oldest son:

> *Between my freshman and sophomore year in high school, I joined the football team. Our team's quarterback was a senior at the time. I knew he would be the starter, but second string was up for grabs. There were three of us in the running. I worked hard to beat out the others for that second-string spot, and also became the holder for field goal kicks.*
>
> *At the end of the summer, right before football season began, I decided I'd rather only play baseball, not football. I asked my dad if I could quit the team. He didn't care whether I played football or not, but he did care that I had earned and committed to play a position and that it was only a month before the start of the season. Dad refused to let me quit. My team was counting on me. I played the whole season. He allowed me to quit the team after the season ended when the coaches had nearly a year to train someone for my jobs. That experience taught me*

that sometimes you have to endure a position or job so as not to leave those who depend on you in a bad situation.

Few people have real integrity today. Instead, they have what I consider *situational ethics.* They will do whatever a situation requires to get or keep them out of trouble. We want more for our children. We don't want them to continue to think like my son did when he was eight years old, trying to avoid taking responsibility for setting his mattress on fire. No, we want our children to grow and mature into the men and women God has called them to be. But that's not an automatic process. To get there, they need us—their dads—to step up and teach them how to have integrity.

Key Points

1. Integrity is a spiritual principle. Having a lack of integrity invites the enemy's curse into children's lives.
2. Integrity must be taught. It is not a trait kids are born with.
3. To teach integrity, you must have integrity yourself. You cannot expect more from your children than you expect from yourself.

Discussion Questions

1. How is integrity lacking in today's society? Give an example.
2. Why is integrity a spiritual issue? How does a lack of it invite Satan's curse into your life or your children's lives?
3. Share a time when you had to correct an issue of integrity with your children. What did you do?
4. Why is it important for dads to have integrity themselves?

Take Action

Watch the news with a critical eye, looking for moments when leaders or spokespeople lack integrity. Consider why they are responding that way. Are they trying to sway their audience or skirt an issue to avoid consequences? What is at stake because of their actions? Let this be a reminder of the importance of teaching integrity to the next generation.

15

Deal with Failure

Create in me a pure heart, O God, and renew a steadfast spirit within me. Do not cast me from your presence or take your Holy Spirit from me. Restore to me the joy of your salvation and grant me a willing spirit, to sustain me.
(Psalm 51:10-12)

I have coached Little League Baseball for 27 years. I know...I completely blame my wife for having so many children. I've seen the good, the bad, and the ugly. The biggest change I've noticed in kids over almost three decades of coaching is how fragile they have become. Yes, *fragile*. They crumble and want to quit when anything goes wrong. I believe this is a direct response to having a lack of fathering.

Children that don't know how to deal with failure don't "swing away". The fear of failure is so strong they would rather not try at all than try and fail. They haven't had a father around to push them out of the nest and teach them to take risks.

Dad, when you teach your children to swing away, you receive the reward of watching them grow up and do something noble with their lives. The courage to swing away isn't an automatic, innate ability. It won't happen unless you push them to try new things and then see them respond to that push, even at the risk of failure. The goal is for them to try.

> If we don't teach our children how to deal with failure, we are stealing their potential and creativity.

With the exception of Jesus, every great man or woman who has accomplished great things or invented revolutionary devices or developed life-changing medicines failed before they succeeded. If we don't teach our children how to deal with failure, we are stealing their potential and creativity. To do that, we must remember some key points.

Love is NOT Dependent on Performance

First and most importantly, don't tie your love to your children's performance. I've talked about this already, but it applies to this lesson, too. I have seen this *sin* so many times at the ball field. Parents won't speak to their child if the child makes a mistake. I don't understand that behavior, and it hurts my heart every time. Children need to know your love is there for them regardless of their performance.

I've told my sons that I'm going to love them regardless

of whether they ever get another hit. They need to hear that over and over again. I demand that they give their best to whatever they choose to do, even if their best doesn't end in a win for them that day. My love and pride for them is not affected by whether they win or lose. Understanding that gives them the security to swing away.

....

...don't tie your love to your children's performance.

....

Isn't that how God the Father relates to us? Aren't we all glad He doesn't base His love for us on our performance? And if that's His example to us, shouldn't we strive to set that same example for our own children?

Deal with Losing

Second, don't let your children take themselves too seriously. Life can be hard, and not everyone wins. Not everyone will have their idea chosen, or their artwork selected, or their effort rewarded. Sometimes they will lose, and that's okay. That's normal. We shouldn't teach kids that they will "win" every time.

As a baseball coach, I can't stand the fact that everyone gets a trophy nowadays. We should teach our children to deal with losing, but we shouldn't reward it. Instead, we should teach them to work harder next time. Life doesn't reward everyone in the same way. To teach our children that everyone gets the same reward is wrong.

We must give our kids a healthy perspective on losing. When we don't, one of two things happen: either they won't try at all, or they will want to win at any cost. Both are damaging. One way to give your children a healthy perspective is to tell them about the times you have failed, struck out, or didn't make the team. Show them that you've lost and are still okay.

Learn to Laugh at Yourself

Third, teach your children to laugh at themselves. In fact, laugh at them yourself. Don't do it in a mean way, of course, but laugh if they fall in the mud and bust it. This is important. Teach them that it's okay to laugh at themselves. Scripture says that laughter does good like a medicine (see Proverbs 17:22).

If red flags are going up in your mind, please understand what I'm saying. If you don't teach your children to laugh at themselves in certain situations, it will crush them when others laugh at them first. And others *will* laugh at them.

Have you ever noticed how some people handle embarrassing situations so well? It's because they learned that they are not perfect, and they'll never be perfect. They can laugh at themselves and move on.

Obviously, there's a healthy difference between teaching them to laugh at themselves and being cruel or demeaning. I encourage you to find that line and allow yourself to laugh within healthy boundaries.

Learn from Your Failures

Help your children evaluate failure and learn from it. Show them that this is a good practice.

One of my greatest frustrations as a pastor is watching people make the same mistakes over and over again. They end up passing it down to their children. We call those mistakes "generational curses". When I see these same curses come up time and again, it breaks my heart. In order to learn, people must be able to see clearly. Those who pass down generational curses *don't* see clearly, which is made evident by their excuses and willingness to blame others for their bad behavior and failures.

I cannot overstate this.

You can't learn until you take responsibility for your actions. When you accept responsibility, there is room for change and to learn and grow. Great men and women throughout history, and even today, have proven that the greatest learning tool we have is failure.

Often times, my boys have gotten mad when trying to achieve something new and said, "I quit! I can't do this!"

I sit them down and take the time to ask them some specific questions:

- *What did you do?*
- *How did it turn out?*
- *What did you learn?*
- *What can you do differently next time?*

We then discuss their answers. It gives them the opportunity to move forward. Failure will happen. That. Is. A. Fact. Those who are able to deal with failure when it comes will be able to move on with their lives. It won't hold them back.

David's Road Map for Dealing with Personal Failure

Psalm 51 was written after King David's big failure. I included a portion of it at the top of this chapter. In it, he gives us the road map for dealing with personal failure. He teaches us to do the following:

1. Admit your failure.
2. Don't blame anyone or anything else for it.
3. Take responsibility. (e.g. "It was my mistake.")
4. Repent and change your thinking.
5. Move on.

This is the same process we must teach our children. We must teach them how to deal with failure so they can succeed in life. Dad, it's up to you.

Key Points

1. Dads must teach their children to deal with failure in a healthy way, or the fear of failure will prevent them from learning to "swing away".
2. Never tie your love for your children to their performance. They should know that you love them regardless of whether they win, lose, or make mistakes.
3. Teach your children that it's okay to lose without rewarding the loss.
4. Teach your children to laugh at themselves so they don't crumble when others laugh at them.
5. Failures provide children with opportunities to learn from their mistakes. You can help your children through that process by asking questions.

Discussion Questions

1. Why is it important to teach your children how to deal with failure?
2. How can the fear of failure prevent your children from fulfilling their callings?
3. How can sharing your own past failures with your children teach your children to deal with theirs?
4. Why do children need to learn how to laugh at themselves? What is the difference between

teaching them to laugh at themselves and demeaning them? Are you leading by example and laughing at yourself in front of them when you make mistakes?

Take Action

At your children's next sporting event, or even at a family or neighborhood game, look at how they deal with failure. Do they quit? Does the fear of failure prevent them from taking necessary risks? Do they want to win at all costs? Let this spark a conversation with them about winning, losing, and dealing with both. Maybe even share with them about a time you lost. Let them see that losing is not the end.

SECTION 4
BUILT FOR PURPOSE

Many young men and women drift from place to place, job to job, hoping and longing for some sense of purpose. Then, they have children and try to find their purpose through their kids, which becomes an incredibly damaging situation for both. The kids end up hating their parents, and the parents are left unfulfilled, still longing for purpose.

That's not the way it's supposed to be because God is all *about* purpose. Throughout the Bible we see the common theme that everything has a purpose. Scripture even says that God made the whales to frolic (see Psalm 104:25-26). If He created whales with a specific purpose, then how much more does He have in store for mankind—the crown jewel of creation?

One of the ways to discover your purpose is to look at what God has given you—your talents, abilities, giftings, and your heart's cry. And, of course, as fathers, God has given us children.

God expects each of us to be responsible caretakers of what He has given us. In other words, my purpose as a father is to raise my children in such a way that they fulfill their own God-given purpose. I want to teach them how to live full lives that bring glory to the Lord. To accomplish this, I know my actions and words are key. I'm not creating purposes for them—that's God's job. He's simply given me the vision for raising them in a way that allows them to fulfill their own unique purposes and, ultimately, change their world.

Acts 13:36 is a verse that inspires me to keep going: "Now when David had served God's purpose in his own generation, he fell asleep; he was buried with his ancestors and his body decayed." Read that verse again. David fulfilled the purpose of God in his generation.

What a wonderful accomplishment!

I long for that to be said about me and my children—and you and your children, too. It all starts at home, raising our children with the ability to make a difference in this world.

16

Help Them Launch

"For I know the plans I have for you,"
declares the LORD, "plans to prosper you and not to
harm you, plans to give you hope and a future."
(Jeremiah 29:11)

I've learned the hard way that mothers and fathers do *not* share the same views on raising children. God made us that way. For instance, every time our children would get ready to either move out on their own or leave for college, my wife would cry and tell them to not go. At the same time, I'd be cheering them on, knowing that it moved them one step closer to getting a *job*. My wife once suggested that we build one big house so that each of our children's families could have their own private wing. My sons and I instantly shot down her idea!

....

Fathers need to help their children launch out
into everything God has for them.

....

Fathers need to help their children launch out into everything God has for them. One way to do that is by speaking into their lives that they have a purpose, something I discussed in detail early on in this book. Psalm 139:14 contains one of my favorite scriptures: "I was there in your mother's womb, skillfully making you" (paraphrased). God has designed each of us, taking great detail in His work.

Then, He said in Jeremiah 29:11, "I know the plans I have for you..." While He was making you and your children, He was thinking about His plans and His thoughts toward you and them. Can you picture the smile on His face as He knitted you together in your mother's womb, and thought of all the good plans He had in store for you?

As I've said, every single one of your children is an arrow you are shooting into the future; how far and how straight each child goes depends a lot on you. Your goal is not to launch them into the destinies you have chosen for them. No, you're helping them discover the destiny *God* has for them.

Some parents try to launch their children into predetermined destinies that *they* want for them. They try to live through their kids. This is a terrible curse to put on a child. Notice I said "curse." When parents try to force their children in a certain direction, their children will either rebel against the parents or submit and be miserable on the inside. Neither is God's will.

Three Foundations for a Successful Launch

This world is filled with people with a crab mentality. If you don't know what I'm talking about, you probably haven't been crabbing on the Gulf of Mexico.

When crabs get trapped, they could easily escape, but they work against each other. When one starts to climb out of the trap, the others will drag it back down. Sadly, people do the same thing. When they feel trapped by the world and unable to fulfill their own destinies, they give up and drag down anyone else who is trying to achieve their destiny, too.

An example of this takes place in the book of Nehemiah 1:1–7:3. Sanballot, Tobiah, and Geshen tried to stop Nehemiah from fulfilling the destiny God had given him of leading his people back to Jerusalem to rebuild the wall around the city. Those men didn't see or understand Nehemiah's call and didn't support it. They didn't have the vision for what he was doing. It was too big and too different for them to comprehend. But that didn't stop Nehemiah, and it shouldn't stop your children either.

....

Your children must have a solid foundation from which to launch or they'll be swept away in a sea of negativity.

....

Your children must have a solid foundation from which to launch or they'll be swept away in a sea of negativity. Here are three things that must be present for your children to successfully launch into their destinies:

1. Develop a Healthy Belief System

People often say, "Just believe in yourself," but that's a totally wrong sentiment. It reflects the world's way of thinking, not God's. Your children must first know that someone else believes *in* them. They must learn over the years that you believe and expect them to succeed.

It's empowering and energizing when your children know you believe in them. This doesn't happen overnight, and they know when you're faking it. That's why, as they're growing up, it's important to give them tasks to do and make them do a good job and finish what they start. It will build their confidence in their abilities and work ethic. In turn, your children will see your confidence in them grow, which will also build their confidence in themselves.

Then, when you truthfully say things like, "I know you can do it," or, "I believe in you," your children will see that your words aren't empty, and that you believe what you're saying. It's like giving them a vitamin B-12 shot. It'll energize them and give them courage to go for their destinies. So, give them chances to prove that you can believe in them.

2. Overcoming Fear of Failure

You will fail.

That's a fact of life. Every person will fail at something. It's the fear of failure, not failure itself, that paralyzes people from fulfilling their destinies.

I mentioned this in chapter 15, but I want to touch on it again. In over 25 years of coaching Little League Baseball, I've seen more and more that kids are afraid to "swing away".

They'll ask, "What if I miss it?" A fear of failure keeps them from swinging at all.

There are so many people with ideas and dreams, but they can only see what might go wrong. Their fear and belief that they're going to fail is worse to them than not trying at all. Fear of failure is stealing their destiny.

Dad, we have to teach our children that all of the great men and women in history had to overcome failure. You will fail. I will fail. Our kids will fail. But that's not the end of the story. The people who get back up and learn from failure are those who live fulfilled lives.

....

Your love and parenting can help drive out
the fear of failure, because they'll know that your
unconditional love means that, no matter what,
you will always love them.

....

Arriving at the end of your life with no regrets is a precious thing. In my line of work, I often hear, "If I had to do it over again…" Well, you don't get to do it over again. You only have one shot. So, go for it. Things won't ever work out if you don't even try. Your children need to understand and believe that overcoming failure is a part of success.

Let me go a little further. Sometimes you must let your children fail and then teach them how to deal with it. That process of failing and getting back up again will give them confidence that they can overcome any obstacle in life. Your love and parenting can help drive out the fear of failure, because they'll know that your unconditional love means that, no matter what, you will always love them. So, teach them to swing away.

From Micah, my oldest son:

> *Football was king in our house. Stories of practice, good throws, and great blocks dominated the dinner table by the time my brothers and I reached high school. My senior year was set up to be special. We had a talented group of seniors and juniors that fit together to make a great team.*
>
> *What was even better? I was going to play with two of my younger brothers, Caleb and Jacob. I was the quarterback, Caleb was the starting receiver, and Jacob was the center. We literally had the potential to have a Hickman snap to a Hickman and throw to a Hickman!*

As the season progressed, we dominated! All 3 Hickman boys were doing well. The team was more special than we had thought, and the whole county knew we had a chance to make it to the Mississippi State Championship. We had one game left against a team that had only won once all season. It looked like an easy win.

In the second quarter, I scrambled out on a pass. No one was open, so I ran. As the defender came up to make the tackle, I planted my left leg and cut hard right. He never touched me, but I collapsed. The bottom of my knee twisted left, and the top half twisted right. I didn't know what happened, but I felt a sharp pain on the inside and back of my knee. I got up to walk it off and collapsed with the first step.

"Please, God, no! Not this year! Not now!"

Dad had made his way to the sideline. "Hey, boy. I'm sorry," he said with tears in his eyes, "but we're gonna make it through this. You hear me?"

The next morning, a family friend who was a doctor gave us the news that I had messed my knee up pretty bad. Not only that, but my bother Caleb was my backup and he had torn his ACL the previous week. Our chances for winning State were slipping away.

I was devastated, but I couldn't stop. I couldn't be the reason our team didn't make it to State. If there was any possibility that I could play, I had to play.

So, Dad made it happen. He ordered a special knee brace and sent me to therapy every day to reduce the swelling and improve my range of motion.

In all the chaos of therapy and trying to convince my coaches that I could play at the championship level, I never shared with anyone how scared I was. I couldn't shake the fear of playing all-out, like nothing was wrong.

By the night of the game, I had proven to the coaches and trainers that I could play. I said the typical motivational things to my team and then went off by myself, afraid my emotions would give me away. My hands were trembling. I couldn't rid myself of the fear; I just couldn't shake it! My heart was racing. I questioned if the brace would hold or if it was possible for me to be the quarterback my team needed me to be. For the first time in my life, I was consumed with the fears of "what if."

About that time, right before kick-off, Dad got permission to come onto the sidelines. He found his way to my side, put his arm around my shoulder pads, and stood with me as we looked across the field together.

He never said a word.

He didn't have to.

Right then, as he had my whole life, he made everything okay. Him simply being there made it okay. No matter what happened from that moment forward, I knew every-

thing was going to be okay. Dad was there.

We went on to win the game...and the conference. However, that game pales in comparison to the moment on the sidelines with my dad. For the first time in my life, I had doubted myself, and, within minutes, Dad was there! I hadn't asked him to be there. Somehow, he had just known that I needed him. To this day, it's my fondest memory.

Someone saw that Hallmark moment and took a picture from the stands. That picture sits on my dresser today. Other people just see my dad with his arm around me. But, to me, it was a defining moment in my life.

3. Discovering God's Calling

Your children must know that God has a purpose and destiny for them, and that the closer they walk with Him the more they will fulfill that destiny. Your children are called to something greater than simply sitting back and living for pleasure or pursuing happiness. Wherever they are, they're called by God to be the light of the world, to bring love to people, and to represent Christ on the earth. Each one is called to be a minister, not necessarily as an occupation, but as an influencer and change agent for God in others' lives. This understanding will help them to not stress over their career choice.

Dad, each of your children has a calling. Understanding that calling will give them a sense that he or she is important and can make a difference in this world. So, let them hear over and over again that life is worth living when they are bringing a little light to it. This will empower them to launch out into the deep.

It's a vital step in helping them become the world changers God desires them to be. They have a purpose, and you are an important part of them fulfilling that purpose. Don't fall asleep on the job, Dad. Your children are depending on you. Help them launch well!

Key Points

1. Every child is an arrow that a dad launches into his or her future.
2. Dads have the responsibility to encourage the dreams and callings of their children, not to determine them.
3. Allowing children to prove that they are trustworthy and hardworking will not only build your confidence in them, but also, in turn, build their confidence in themselves as they see your confidence in them grow.
4. Failure is inevitable; so, teach your children to "swing away".
5. God has a calling for every person, and children must be told this repeatedly. It is this knowledge that gives life meaning and purpose.

Discussion Questions

1. Why is it a curse for a parent to try to set a child's destiny?
2. What is a "crab" mentality? Have you seen this practiced? Has it happened to you? Why must we teach our children to overcome the crab mentality of others?

3. Why is believing in yourself not enough? Why is it important for your kids to see that you believe in them?
4. Do you agree that failure is inevitable? Why or why not? How can you prepare your children to handle failure well?
5. How can you teach your children that God has a destiny for them? Why is the pursuit of happiness a poor goal in life?

Take Action

Begin talking to your children about their destinies. Even if they are too young to talk about specific plans, begin teaching them what destiny is and reinforcing the knowledge that their destiny is God-given. If they are older, then begin talking to them about the calling God has begun revealing to them. Make it clear that they are world changers and created for more than useless pursuits of pleasure.

17

Your Children Are World Changers

"You are the light of the world. ...Let your light shine before others, that they may see your good deeds and glorify your Father in heaven."
(Matthew 5:14,16)

I deal with so many people who are dissatisfied with their lives. I can't tell you how many times I've heard people say, "If I had to do it over again, I would change things." Unfortunately, they don't get that opportunity. None of us do. If we want a different outcome, we must change things *now*.

God has called all of us to be salt and light (see Matthew 5:13-16). Light has an immediate and drastic effect on a dark room. It dispels the darkness and makes things visible. It's a dramatic change. In the same way, God has called us all to be world changers.

I've told my boys a thousand times, "You may not be able to change *the* world, but you can change *your* world."

Dad, your presence alone changes your children's worlds. Regardless of whether you were available to them in their early years, you can commit to being there now. So be there. Play with them. Wrestle with them. Get dirty with them. Say the things they need to hear. Sacrifice your wants and desires to change their world.

There is no substitute for a dad's presence.

Let me say that again: *there is absolutely no substitute for a dad being there.*

You are irreplaceable. Starting at a young age, your children need you to show them how to change their worlds. Take them with you when you go to help someone move, to deliver food to someone, to cut grass for a single mother, to pray for someone, or to pay for someone else's washing/drying at a laundromat.

I hope you're seeing the pattern here. You need to model being a world changer in front of them so that the example comes from you first. By doing so, you're training them how to look outside of themselves and meet the needs of those in their own world. That's exactly what Jesus did, and He was the greatest world changer of all time!

Let's take a closer look at two things your children must understand to be true world changers:

1. Show Them That What They Do Matters

Many people live with a "lost-in-the-crowd" mentality. They believe it doesn't matter whether or not they're present. What a crippling thought! Having this sort of mentality allows for a selfish life.

YOUR CHILDREN ARE WORLD CHANGERS

As we saw earlier, the Bible says clearly in Psalm 139 that God made you just the way you are and has a plan for you. And Jesus made it clear that His plan involves changing the world.

....

> You must instill in your children that they are not simply here to live. They are not here by accident. They're not here only to do the best they can, or merely get by. All these attitudes are a cancer that will steal their destinies and cause them to endure life instead of changing it for the better.

....

You must instill in your children that they are not simply here to live. They are not here by accident. They're not here only to do the best they can, or merely get by. All these attitudes are a cancer that will steal their destinies and cause them to endure life instead of changing it for the better.

Light was given for a specific purpose: to chase back the darkness. Salt was also given for a specific purpose: to flavor and preserve. The Bible says that if salt has lost its flavor then what good is it (see Matthew 5:13)? You toss it out. That describes a number of people, doesn't it? They feel like they're merely going through life, feeling tossed aside. But we were made with a purpose—and being salt and light to this lost world is part of that purpose.

Dad, talk to your children about how there is no one else in this world exactly like them, that what God has created them to do is designed specifically for them, and that no one else can fulfill their destinies for them. They are called to change the world, not endure it (or complain about it). There's not a single person on the face of this earth who can do exactly what they can do.

From Samuel, my sixth oldest son:

> *Day in and day out, my dad showed us through his example how to be men of character, men who keep their word, work hard, give honor where honor is due, fight for the weak, never quit, and stay true to who we are. It is because of this that my brothers and I are confident that we can indeed be world changers. We know that no matter what this world throws at us, we can rise to the occasion and say, "I can do it. Follow me." With every lesson he taught us, he instilled a piece of a puzzle in us that would undoubtedly shape the men we were becoming. Because of my father, I am confident and grounded in the man that I am.*

2. Small Things Can Make a Big Difference

In the kingdom of God, small things can make a difference. Jesus talked about how mustard seed-sized faith can move mountains. Far too many people dismiss the impact of something as simple as a random act of kindness.

It reminds me of when my wife was on bed rest while pregnant with one of our children. People would come by and bring her magazines to help her pass the time. While reading one of them, she found an article about a town in New York that came together to build a park. It sparked a vision in her and she said to me, "We need a park like that here."

About a year later, hundreds of volunteers in our city gathered together to build a park for our community. One little park in our small city may not seem like a big deal, but it turned out to be just that. My oldest boys worked alongside the volunteers every day and witnessed what happened next with their own eyes.

TV station journalists and magazine publishers started showing up. Eventually ten other towns and cities in our state, and several in other states, grabbed hold of the vision and started building their own parks, too. Because our small city took hold of the opportunity to launch a vision, our entire region changed. I'm so thankful our boys got to see this up close!

You never know what God will do and how far He will take a vision when you decide to be a world changer.

In another instance, I watched one of my sons raise money for two water wells in Africa. Another of my sons became a high school teacher and coach because he believes he can make a difference in kids' lives. My other sons are serving at church and giving their lives away in other ways—all because they each know that if they take a step toward changing their world, God can use it to perform miracles.

> Simple things under God's anointing can send ripples into the future. But whatever you do, start today.

Dad, start acknowledging and reaffirming to your children that they have in them what it takes to be a world changer. It's okay to start small. Simple things under God's anointing can send ripples into the future. But whatever you do, start today.

My son and daughter-in-law, Jacob and Krista, were living in an older apartment when a couple in our church offered to help them update it. The couple said they could replace cabinets, put in new flooring, and more—all for free. Jacob was uncomfortable with not paying for the work that was going into their home, so he seized the opportunity to talk to the husband about his concerns.

The man stopped him before too long into the conversation and asked if he could tell Jacob a story. He shared with Jacob how his great-grandfather had been a poor sharecropper in Louisiana with two sons. The man's simple income had been so little that he couldn't afford the expense of doctors or medicine. His oldest son had come down with an illness that could've been treated but claimed the boy's life instead.

The son's death shook the family, especially the father, so he decided to move the family to Pearl River County in south Mississippi. There, the unthinkable happened: his second son became sick and medicine still cost more than he could afford.

Someone had told him about a man at a pharmacy in the city of Picayune who might help. So, with his son's life and death on the line, the father took a chance and traveled to Picayune to talk to that man. True to what he had been told, the pharmacist gave him the medicine he needed at no charge. The boy's life was saved.

Standing across from Jacob, the husband concluded with tears streaming down his face, "The boy whose life was saved was my grandfather, and the man who gave him the medicine was your great-grandfather. I can't help but help you."

Every time I think of that story, a shiver goes down my spine.

You never know what one act of kindness will release into the future, so teach your children to be world changers. Teach them to be people who make a difference right where they are. Let them see you do it. Let them be part of the action. Let them see how God can use their deeds, no matter how small. They may not change the whole world, but they can certainly change theirs.

Key Points

1. Dads need to teach their children—through words and actions—to make their world a better place wherever they go.
2. As Christians, we're called to do more than live self-focused lives. We're to be salt and light in all we do. Your children need to hear and see that in action.
3. One act of kindness can have a long-lasting impact on the world.

Discussion Questions

1. How can selfishness derail a person's calling?
2. Why is mentoring so important when teaching your children to be world changers?
3. In what ways can you teach your children to change their world?
4. Share a time when someone's act of kindness affected you.

Take Action

Look for acts of kindness that you can do with your children. Commit to doing one or more this month. Need ideas? Consider mowing a neighbor's yard, picking up trash in your city, or volunteering at a retirement center, veteran's center, or your church.

18

Create a Rite of Passage

When I was a child, I talked like a child, I thought like a child, I reasoned like a child. When I became a man, I put the ways of childhood behind me.
(1 Corinthians 13:11)

In the 1950s, the psychology community invented the word "adolescence", and it has been a curse on our country ever since. Before then, a person was referred to as either a child or an adult.

There is nothing sadder than watching a 30- or 40-year-old act like a teenager, stuck in that mystical stage called *adolescence*. The carnage that is currently the American family is a direct result of men and women producing children they have no desire or ability to properly take care of. These men and women don't know how to handle their finances, pay their bills, live on a budget, or deal with problems maturely. They are adolescents who live for the moment and try to escape any pain at all.

The divorce rate reflects this: We break up with families like we break up with boyfriends or girlfriends. Men and women jump in and out of marriage, producing children who end up suffering from a lack of identity. School systems end up raising children instead of educating them. Addictions to alcohol and drugs skyrocket because what looked like fun became a trap. These are problems that belong to all of us. We need adults to be adults and make adult decisions.

> I believe we need to call our children into adulthood.

How to Hold a Ceremony Celebrating Adulthood

To help, the Lord led me to create a rite of passage ceremony for my children. Every great society has a rite of passage from childhood to adulthood except for ours, but I believe we need to call our children into adulthood. Of course, they'll continue to grow and learn from their mistakes, but there should be an event that marks their "crossing over" into the next stage of growing up—an event and time that they can look forward to. In our family, we've seen a significant difference in the level of maturity in each of our boys after their rite of passage.

How We Perform a Rite of Passage

We hold the event outside. Friends and family are invited to participate. Men who I believe meet the biblical require-

CREATE A RITE OF PASSAGE

ments of a godly man form two rows and face each other with enough room between them for a person to walk. Two men, one on either side of the aisle, hold a string or cord between them. I (as the father) stand at the end of the path, and my son stands at the beginning.

I spend a few moments welcoming everyone who has come to witness the rite of passage. Then, I share a few things about what it means to step into manhood and how proud I am of my young man. Finally, I call him by name and ask him this specific question, "Are you ready to step into manhood?"

His first step down the path is met with the cord hanging between the first two men. He breaks the cord. Those men come prepared to share a statement, scripture, or word with my son. Once they finish sharing, they lay hands on him and pray blessings over him.

Each set of men has a different character trait that I have asked them to speak to (e.g. godly character, a man after God's own heart, etc.). The traits are based on the qualities I believe a godly man possesses.

After each step is taken, I ask my son again, "Are you willing to take the next step into manhood?" Upon his agreement, the process is repeated.

1. Step forward.
2. Break the cord.
3. Receive the sharing of a statement,

scripture, or word from two men.
4. Receive prayer.
5. Declare that he is ready to take the next step into manhood.

Once he has passed through each pair of men and broken their cord, he arrives at the end of the path where I am standing. This is where I present him with his own study Bible, and pronounce blessings on him as his father. Then, all the men in line approach and lay hands on him, and together we pray and welcome my son into manhood.

Then, we celebrate with a party.

I am sure if I had a daughter, I would change some aspects of the ceremony to fit her path into womanhood, but the principle would be the same.

> The spiritual ramifications of a Rite of Passage ceremony for your children will resonate throughout their lives.

Call Your Children into Adulthood

We need adults calling their children into adulthood.

The spiritual ramifications of a rite of passage ceremony for your children will resonate throughout their lives. My

CREATE A RITE OF PASSAGE

wife and I have noticed how much this ceremony has affected each of our boys' decisions and worldview. Not only were they affected mentally and spiritually, but also in the way that they perceived themselves. After they moved into adulthood, they saw themselves as people created with a need to *contribute* to society, not simply *take* from it. The transformation we've seen in each of our children is beyond words.

You don't have to do it this way, of course, but I strongly encourage you to hold a rite of passage ceremony with your kids. With your blessing, they can boldly and securely step into adulthood. Your children realizing "I became an adult when my dad told me I was an adult" makes an immeasurable difference in their lives. It allows them to leave so-called *adolescence* behind and calls them to "put away childish things." It transforms boys into world-changing men and girls into world-changing women.

Key Points

1. The term *adolescence* was introduced in the 1950s and has since prevented children from taking the necessary step into adulthood.
2. Most cultures have a rite of passage ceremony for children as a way of calling them into adulthood.
3. The rite of passage ceremony does two things: A) it allows a child to publicly declare that he (or she) is an adult and to take their first step into adulthood; and, B) it allows the child's father to bless and pray over his child and publicly declare that the child is an adult.

Discussion Questions

1. Why is the idea of adolescence detrimental to kids?
2. What is a rite of passage ceremony and why is it important?

Take Action

Plan your children's rite of passage ceremony, making sure to include a blessing from you to them. Whether you follow my ceremony exactly or create your own, I strongly encourage you to make this a practice for each of your children.

FINAL THOUGHTS

I pray this book has helped you capture a vision for your role as a father. The impact you have on your children—now and for the rest of their lives—can't be ignored, overlooked, or discounted.

It's because of you, Dad, that they will learn who they are and what part God has called them to play in this world. It's because of you that your children will have the courage and perseverance to launch out into their destinies and do what only they can do.

Your children have so much to offer. God has equipped them with unique gifts and talents. No one else on earth is designed with their exact mixture of perspective, insight, and life experience. Just imagine what the Lord can do with and through their lives!

But their success is not automatic. Many people never live up to their potential. Without a dad's presence and attention, the enemy will work overtime to weaken them and minimize the contributions they can make to the world.

Don't let that happen to your children.

You don't have to be the perfect father—only our heavenly Father is capable of that. But you can be the father your children need you to be, the father the Lord has called *you* to be. You can be the father that gives them their identity, teaches them to value the right things, and disciplines them in love so they grow into strong, confident, selfless adults who understand their place in the world. You can be the father that helps them launch successfully into the destiny God has for them.

Never doubt how much they need you. Your children are your greatest legacy and the most valuable arrows you'll ever launch.

Now it's up to you, a true warrior with vision.

Shoot them well.

Shoot them strong.

Shoot them toward their God-ordained destiny.

You are *Irreplaceable!*